SERIOUS MONEY

SERIOUS MONEY

Straight Talk about Investing for Retirement

Richard A. Ferri, CFA

Published by Portfolio Solutions, LLC
Troy, Michigan

Printed in the United States of America

ISBN 0-9672943-0-4
SAN 299-9242

Published by Portfolio Solutions, LLC
4693 Fairmont Drive, Troy, MI 48089

Editing and page design by Griffith Publishing
Cover design by Arbor Graphic Design
Cover photo by Dennis Greaney Photography

To my loving wife, Daria, for all
your patience and support.

Contents

PART III Closing the Performance Gap

A Note from the Author

For the past eleven years, I have been helping individual investors achieve their financial goals. When I first came into the investment business, I was very naive. Like most people, I believed stockbrokers and other investment advisors were skilled professionals who knew things about the markets that other people did not know, and they made a lot of money for their clients and themselves. So, when I started bringing on clients, I recommended stocks that were followed by the research department and touted by the experienced brokers in the office. How could I go wrong?

Well, it didn't take long for me to realize that our stock picks were no better than those of any other firms, and many times much worse. I realized that analysts and brokers have ulterior motives for recommending certain stocks to their clients, mainly to generate commissions and investment banking fees. Making money for clients based on our research is a noble thought, but that only happened by chance.

I searched for a better way to invest money, and it wasn't long before I discovered money managers and mutual funds. These outside professional investors made all the stock decisions in the account, and I collected a commission on the transactions. This made perfect sense. Managers had an incentive to make money for their clients so they could collect larger fees. In addition, managers were well educated and articulate. Their colorful marketing materials also made for an easy sale. Surely this was the way for my clients to achieve superior returns.

Alas, managers, too, were an illusion. Mutual funds and private money managers as a group were no more capable of achieving high returns than throwing darts at that stock pages of *The Wall Street Journal*. A few managers did achieve respectable returns, meaning their results came close to the return of the market. But overall, they were a disappointment. It was time to move on.

The next stop was totally new. If success could not be found in the stock market, perhaps the futures pits would prove more fruitful. Hedge funds seemed like rocket science, and the industry attracted an extraordinary group of people. Mathematicians and physicists that designed Star Wars weaponry during the Cold War were now working on Wall Street designing money machines. They sat in a room observing every wiggle in the financial markets looking for trading opportunities. These smart people could be hired to manage money for my clients, which was certain to lead to wealth.

Well, there were certainly a lot of wiggles generated in those accounts, and some people actual made money. My firm made money, the rocket scientists made money, I made money, but my clients didn't make much money. The fees and expenses of the hedge funds wiped out most of their gains.

Frustrated, I decided to manage the money myself. If the analysts, money mangers, and rocket scientists could not beat the markets, surely there was someone who could, and that someone might as well be me. I realized I needed more education, which took me back to academia. Over a seven-year period I achieved a Chartered Financial Analyst (CFA) designation and Master of Finance degree, while continuing to work full time in the investment field. In addition, I read dozens of books and hundreds of research reports on the subject of investing, trying to find the secret to success.

This educational barrage began to pay off when I realized I was searching for a false prophet. My initial idea was to find a strategy that "beat the markets" so my clients could accumulate more wealth. However, I found very little evidence to support that thesis. Most academic studies were flush with data to the contrary. The more I studied the data, the more I realized that no such "superior" strategy existed, at least not one that was available to the public. The more people tried to beat the markets, the further behind they fell.

In reviewing hundreds of actual portfolios over the years, it became very clear to me that almost every investor would have been further ahead financially had they simply put their money into low cost, market matching *index funds*. I expect the same result will be repeated for generations to come. On average, individual investors will accumulate wealth faster and safer if they simply accept the returns of the markets, rather than try to beat them. I have joined a small but growing number of independent investment advisors who recommend index funds to their clients. It is one strategy that has a high probability for success in the future. Quoting Warren Buffett once more, "I'd rather be certain of a good return than hopeful of a great one."

Introduction

Serious Money: Straight Talk About Investing for Retirement

We would all like to be successful investors, yet few people achieve a fair return on their investments given the risks they take. Misconceptions about the financial markets cause large reductions in returns. What are these common mistakes and how can people change their approach to eliminate them? Typical investment books promote strategies designed to beat the markets. Those ideas may sound good and look good on paper, but study after study concludes that "beat the market" advice almost always fails and ends up hampering retirement savings in the long term.

Serious Money offers a better alternative. This book promotes a philosophy that leads to superior wealth by "indexing" the markets' return. Indexing is an investment style designed to match the performance of the markets rather than trying to beat them. By using an indexing strategy, most investors will achieve higher returns on their investment portfolios without adding risk. One way to achieve the return of a market is to use market-matching "index funds." Several mutual fund companies offer index funds. They are also available for a variety of markets, including the U.S. stock market, the international stock market, the corporate bond market, and other markets worldwide. Investors who embrace an indexing strategy will, in the long run, be further ahead than if they listen to popular investment advice and try to "beat the street."

There is a big difference between perception and reality on Wall Street. A carefully crafted perception persists that it is easy to beat the markets by following the recommendations of stockbrokers, analysts, magazines, books, newsletters, and other "expert" advice. Unfortunately, little evidence supports this belief. In fact, nearly every major academic study concludes the opposite. Beat-the-market strategies sold to the public *en masse* eventually backfire, causing below-market results overall. The allure of beating the market has created huge profits for those selling investment products and services while investors buying those products have experienced a large gap between their return and the return of the markets.

This book includes dozens of references to little-known academic studies. Top colleges and universities publish a tremendous amount of information that is useful to individual investors. Several Nobel Prize-winning economists contribute to this body of knowledge on a regular basis. Unfortunately, much of the research remains trapped in academia for two basic reasons. First, the work is often complex and technical, making it difficult for the average reader to decipher. Second, much of the research refutes the marketing claims of large investment firms. Professors on a limited budget have difficulty competing against the marketing power of Wall Street.

Serious Money explains an investment approach that leads to greatest opportunity for a secure retirement. By understanding the financial services industry and by learning the real drivers behind investment success, you can construct an efficient portfolio that meets your retirement needs.

This book begins with an explanation of the retirement problem facing America and tells why every working adult needs to learn about effective investment strategies. With Social Security and corporate pensions diminishing, each person will rely more and more on his or her own investment savvy to ensure a financial security in retirement. The problem is so critical that some Generation Xers believe they are more likely to be abducted by a UFO than collect from the Social Security system.

Part I, Chapters 2-6:
The Performance Gap

The remainder of the book is divided into three distinct parts. Part I provides the hard facts about the publics lack of investment success in the financial markets, and explains the reasons for the shortfall. Most people are not fully aware of how their investments are performing or how they compare to the appropriate market benchmark. Surveys show wide dispersion between perceived returns and actual results. One example was the scandal surrounding the famous Beardstown Ladies (*Beardstown Ladies' Common-Sense Investment Guide*, New York: Simon & Schuster, 1995).

How large is the performance gap between investor returns and market returns? The average individual investor achieves about *half* the return of the markets they invest in. Studies documenting this phenomenon go back as far as the early 1900s. Recently, a major research project of mutual fund investors conducted by an independent company confirmed the earlier findings. Having personally analyzed the returns of hundreds of individual portfolios, I find performance is definitely lacking. Individual investors are not achieving performance anywhere close to the average profit gains of the firms they invest in.

Why does the performance gap exist? Three chapters in Part I summarize three major reasons for this gap. First, the cost of investing is considerable for the public. Whether they realize it or not, investors spend on average two percent per year for portfolio management. Commissions, fees, and other charges have a direct impact on investment results. Second, market timing errors reduce performance. As investors try to guess the future direction of the markets, they attempt to buy low and sell high. This may sound appealing in theory, but there is no academic evidence that any market timing strategy works. Third, people want to be winners, and they want to own winning investments, so they tend to chase strategies that have recently beaten the markets. Unfortunately, this strategy, called *chasing the hot dot*, is the single greatest barrier to success. As investors switch from one investing fad to another, they significantly reduce their long-term results.

Part II, Chapters 7-10: Investment Experts and Other Barriers to Success

Why do people consistently make investment mistakes such as market timing? One answer lies in an analysis of the investment industry. *Serious Money* Part II takes a hard look at the antics of the players on Wall Street and the sellers of investment advice. The industry does an adequate job of educating the public about basic investment concepts and retirement needs, but it does a poor job of executing those concepts. Having spent ten years as a stockbroker at two national firms, I am familiar with the misleading sales tactics used on Wall Street, and the potential of the products sold. Do not confuse the goals of your financial advisor with your own. While many honest and ethical people work in the field, as a whole the industry exists to make money *from* you, not *for* you.

The public is often confused by the role of financial planners, stockbrokers, and other advisors who render investment advice. Most of these people sell investment products and services and are paid a commission or fee for doing so. The title of "Vice President" and other fancy names are earned by reaching a sales quota, not as a result of experience or client satisfaction. There are few requirements needed to become a financial advisor and virtually no academic background is necessary. As a result, many advisors have only a limited understanding of the markets and the investment products they recommend. Although many people believe their advisor is an investment expert, this is typically far from the truth.

The mass media have taken Wall Street by storm. Hundreds of magazines, TV shows, radio talk shows, and Internet sites pump out investment advice on a regular basis. Is any of this information worth following? The perception is that the advice helps people invest effectively for retirement and other goals. In reality, the information concentrates on short-term trading strategies that lead to low returns. Realize that the media is not in the advice business but in the advertising business. They sell advertising space to mutual funds, brokerage firms, and other distributors of financial products and services. Your success as an investor is irrelevant to the goals of the mass media.

With more than 400 mutual-fund companies and over 10,000 mutual funds on the market, investing in mutual funds has become a national phenomenon. However, the mutual fund industry has many ghosts in the closet. Few people know much about the funds they invest in or about the mutual fund industry in general. The last chapter in Part II explains some interesting and disturbing facts about the industry. In the never-ending battle for investor attention, many companies use questionable sales practices, and promote short-term investment strategies. This lowers investor performance and increases the tax burden.

Part III, Chapters 11-16: Closing the Performance Gap

Part III of this book offers a solution for achieving a fair return on your retirement savings. It begins with a brief historical review of the stock and bond markets plus an estimate of the returns expected in the future. The performance of the markets over the next twenty years is likely to be more challenging than for the past twenty years.

Investing in the stock market is best accomplished through indexing. This method involves the purchase of securities that are designed to produce the return of a market index, such as the Dow Jones Industrial Average. Several low cost index funds are available through a number of mutual fund companies. An investor should build a globally diversified portfolio of low-cost index funds and maintain that mix for a very long time. Indexing the global equity markets keeps investment costs low and eliminates the need to chase popular strategies.

The bond market offers investors a variety of low-cost options. People can purchase individual bonds or invest in bond index funds. Part III includes simple strategies explaining each method. Purchasing individual tax-free municipal bonds offers a great advantage for high net worth investors. In complex markets, such as high yield bonds or mortgages, investors should rely on low-cost index funds.

We all have different ideas of what "retirement" means. For some people it means no work at all; for others it means cutting back from a full-time occupation.

Nevertheless, every retiree should know approximately how much money they need at retirement and develop a savings plan to meet that goal. The annual income from this nest egg should be large enough to fill in the gap left by diminishing pensions and Social Security.

One step in the financial plan is to decide how much to invest in stocks and bonds. This *asset allocation* decision is based in part on the *mathematical assumptions* of the retirement goal plus an investor's attitude toward risk. What makes a plan work is the discipline to maintain a consistent allocation over a long period of time and during all market conditions. If people take too much risk in their portfolio, they are likely to abandon the investment plan during adverse market conditions, which will lead to lower long-term results.

Tax planning is an essential ingredient in any investment plan and is covered as a separate chapter in this book. Investors should use tax advantage retirement accounts and purchase tax-efficient investments whenever possible. The less you pay Uncle Sam, the more you have working on your behalf.

The last chapter includes a review of the book's main points and a case study of how a couple invested their portfolio using the ideas outlined in Part III. Achieving a fair return is not difficult. The ideas presented in this book are logical, easy to understand, and lead to greater wealth. Warren Buffett once said, "You don't need to be a rocket scientist. Investing is not a game where the guy with the 160 IQ beats the guy with 130 IQ."

Three Appendices

Serious Money ends with three appendices. Appendix I provides the formulas needed to calculate an investment return. Every investor should keep track of returns on a regular basis and compare the returns to an appropriate market benchmark. Appendix II is for individual stock investors. It explains why stock investing is only a hobby and should be treated as such. It also explores the relationship between brokerage firms and investment banking clients. Appendix III provides background information about the over-sold use of asset allocation models. Advisors who sell products based on simplistic risk-tolerance questionnaires and asset allocation tools create more harm than good.

Chapter 1

The Importance of Saving for Retirement

Most of us have a pretty clear idea of the world we want.
What it takes is an understanding of how to go about
getting it.

—Hugh Gibson

A dramatic change is taking place across working America. People are realizing that traditional sources of retirement income from pension plans and Social Security are quickly diminishing. Soon all retirees will be dependent on personal savings or work for a majority of their income. This means Americans must save an adequate amount prior to retirement and make intelligent investment decisions with those savings. In a sense, the future of America rests on the ability of workers to save and invest properly.

Unfortunately, most investors do not have the information or experience needed to make the best investment choices, and that includes personal financial advisors as well. We are inundated with investment information and advice from hundreds of sources, each promising higher or safer returns. As time goes by, the chore of selecting suitable investments has become increasingly difficult as markets expand around the world and the burgeoning financial services industry expands with it. Wise investors try to develop a simple investment strategy that makes the process simple and profitable.

Before we look at the problems and solutions pertaining to retirement savings, this chapter provides some background information on individual investors. Many of the terms explained below are used throughout the chapters in this book.

Who are Individual Investors?

The financial services industry typically divides investors in two categories: institutional and individual.

Institutional investors include banks, trust companies, mutual fund companies, insurance companies, corporate and government pension funds, endowments, charitable organizations, and other entities with large pools of money. Institutions hire professional money managers full time to evaluate investment opportunities and manage portfolios. Basically, they manage *other people's money.*

In contrast, individual investors are responsible for managing their own money and possibly the funds of a small pension plan, personal trust, or family estate. They are not professional investors and are not paid for managing investment portfolios or evaluating investment options. Most individual investors control assets of less than $100,000. As a direct result of their smaller size, individuals tend to pay much more for investment products and services but typically get a lot less for their money. The wonderful returns you have been hearing about on Wall Street are not those experienced by the average individual investor. Part I of this book explains that fact in full detail.

It is worth noting that stockbrokers, financial planners, insurance agents, and other personal investment advisors are *not* institutional investors, although they may manage other people's money. These personal advisors generally act as *middlemen* between individuals and institutional investors and are really product salespeople. They are typically paid a fee or commission for selling the products and services of institutions such as mutual funds or variable annuities.

How We Will Pay for Retirement

Americans are becoming increasingly responsible for their own financial well being in retirement. The prospect of living off a company pension and Social Security check is rapidly diminishing. Retirees are already relying less on traditional sources of income and more on savings and part-time work. For future retirees the situation will get worse. The desire to build a large nest egg for retirement has been replaced by the need to build one for survival.

In the 1960s company retirement checks and payments from Social Security accounted for over fifty percent of a retiree's income. By 1992 those traditional sources of income had dropped to less than thirty percent. When millions of baby boomers begin to retire in 2010, income from traditional sources may approach ten percent. The shortfall in income must be made up through a combination of personal savings and part-time work. Those who do not save for retirement may find their Golden Years are spent flipping burgers at the Golden Arches.

How People Will Pay for Retirement

	Traditional Pension	Federal Pro-grams	Personal Savings	Part-time Work
1992	8%	19%	46%	27%
2029	4%	7%	48%	41%

Source: Fortune Magazine

The Growth of Individual Retirement Accounts

America's answer to the retirement savings problem seems to be company-sponsored 401(k)s and similar plans. Over 270,000 corporations offer employees a 401(k) tax-deferred savings plan and thousands of public employers offer 403(b) plans to hospital workers, teachers, and government employees. Contributions are made to these plans through regular payroll deductions and some employers match a portion of those savings.[1] According to the Department of Labor, over forty million workers are covered under a 401(k) or similar plan. At the beginning of 1999, there was more than $1.0 trillion invested in these plans, and that amount is expected to grow to $2.0 trillion by 2003.[2]

---

1. Over 90% of large plans have an employer match, according to the Bureau of Labor Statistics, *Data for Large Businesses,* 1995; and Buck Consultants, *Survey Report on Plan Design,* Ninth Edition, 1997
2. Spectrum Group-Access Research (Windsor, CT)

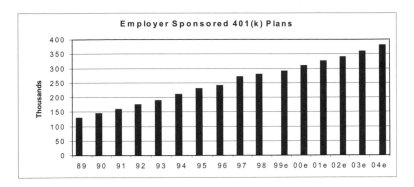

In addition to 401(k) type plans, Individual Retirement Accounts (IRAs) have also flourished. This has happened for a couple of reasons. One is employee turnover and the second is tax law changes.

Only a generation ago, a large percent of workers spent most of their adult life at one company, retiring after decades of service with a gold timepiece and a monthly pension. Times have changed. *The Current Population Survey* shows workers have become much more transient.[3] Back in 1983 the average middle-aged male worker stayed on the job for thirteen years; by 1996 that was down to ten years. Women average only seven years at each company where they work. The decrease in service time is a result of corporate downsizing, productivity gains, and a fundamental shift in the economy from a manufacturing base to a service base.

The increase in job turnover has resulted in tens of millions of IRAs. When a person leaves a company, they normally roll the pension plan into an IRA to avoid taxes. This rollover of pension money has led to a large increase in IRA accounts. As people move from one job to another, they have much more to worry about than investing this money. As a result, many workers have

3. Diane Cripell, *American Demographics*, April 1997. In her article Cripell cited the Employee Benefit Research Institute as the source of the statistics.

IRA rollovers scattered all over the place in various mutual funds and banks. Many of these IRAs are not in optimal investments. This money can remain stagnant for years, earning returns below the market and resulting in less money at retirement.

In addition to rollover IRAs from pension accounts, many people have *contributory* IRAs. Prior to 1987 all wage earners could contribute up to $2,000 per year pre-tax into an IRA. Congress changed the tax law in the late 1980s, and many people lost the opportunity to contribute. However, the accounts still exist. Like IRA rollovers, much of this money is neglected, stashed away in some forgotten investment.

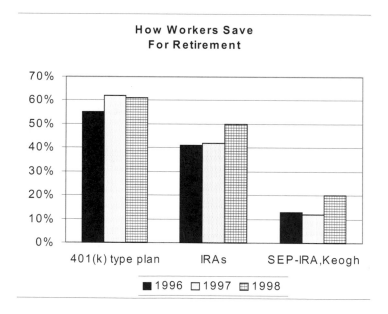

By 1997 there were over 140 million IRA accounts nationwide holding $500 billion in assets.[4] However, this did not stop Congress from creating new IRAs. The Taxpayer Relief Act of 1997 included two new accounts

---

4. Department of Labor statistic, 1997

called the Roth IRA and the Educational IRA. Under both plans new accounts need to be open, adding to the mountain of existing paperwork. Both the Roth and Educational IRAs have gotten a lot of public interest.

Lots of Accounts to Keep Track Of

Since we are involved in so many accounts, it is not hard to understand how investors can lose track of their investments. Putting all this information in one place and analyzing it as one portfolio is a beginning step toward increasing your investment results. I recommend using a spreadsheet program like Microsoft Excel® or a financial planning program like Quicken® to help organize the data. Some Internet web sites offer a free service that allows you to type in account positions and track the portfolios on a daily basis.

The Challenge

During his 1999 State of the Union Address, President Bill Clinton acknowledged the impending crisis in Social Security. As Americans become more responsible for their own retirement income, investment skills must improve. Contrary to popular belief, there is no secret formula to investing in the markets. This book dispels many myths about investing and the investment process. A secure retirement is gained by following a few simple rules and sticking with them for a lifetime. The strategies outlined in Part III of this book are simple, low cost, and offer a tax-friendly solution to saving for retirement.

PART I

The Performance Gap

Chapter 2

Investor Results: Perception versus Reality

The easiest thing of all is to deceive one's self; for what a man wishes, he generally believes to be true.
—Demosthenes

Saving money for retirement is an important part of every financial plan. At least as important is the rate of return you earn on your retirement savings. Without an adequate return on investment, decades of saving may not be enough to maintain your lifestyle in retirement.

This book is dedicated to increasing your rate of return by educating you on the investment process and the investment industry. The ideas presented in this book are not new, or exciting, or revolutionary. They are simple, logical, and non-speculative. They have their roots in academia, not in the marketing departments of the large Wall Street institutions.

A large gap exists between *investment* returns and *investor* returns. Studies document that a big difference exists between *personal* performance in the markets and the returns of the markets themselves. This chapter focuses on elements of your personal investment performance that you may not have considered or have not recently addressed.

When most people talk about investment returns, they generally discuss how the stock market is performing or how a particular mutual fund they own is faring. Few people talk about their total long-term results. Generally, the public has only a vague idea of their personal investment performance. In many cases, individual investors believe they are earning at least a market return in their money, when in reality, they are receiving far less than that.

The problem of investor performance receives little attention in the press but has caught the eye of the Securities and Exchange Commission (SEC). There is talk of requiring mutual fund companies to report *individual* performance to investors rather than the *theoretical* returns listed in the newspaper. Until the requirements change, the only way you can know your actual return is to calculate it yourself (see Appendix I). Do not rely on stockbrokers or other financial advisors to calculate your return for you. Most advisors are paid commissions or fees for their investment advice. The quality of that advice is questionable because of issues involved in measuring performance and the way the advisor is compensated for giving advice.

Wise investors will check the results of their portfolio on a regular basis and compare it to an appropriate market index. Monitoring portfolio results will help expose the large performance gap that exists between the return of the markets and the return to investors. We will discuss in future chapters how investment costs, market-timing errors, and portfolio turnover contribute to the performance gap, and how you can easily eliminate most of the gap between perceived and actual earning for your portfolio.

An Introduction to Investor Returns

It is no secret that stock and bond markets have returned unprecedented gains since the early 1980s. Low inflation and the lengthy economic expansion have provided a windfall for investors in financial assets. Though the performance of the financial markets have been exceptional, the average individual investor has had a difficult time capturing those returns. According to DALBAR Financial Services, the average stock and bond mutual fund investor achieved only about *half* the returns of the markets they invested in during the period[5] (see Chapter 3 for details on the DALBAR data and similar studies).

Having personally calculated hundreds of individual investor returns over the years, I concur with the DALBAR data. Individual investors have not come close to the returns of the stock and bond markets they invest in—and the trend continues to this day.

Obviously, in any study of investor returns, no two people achieve exactly the same results, and the range is wide. However, as a group the performance of individual investors is remarkably low. There may be a segment of the population that actually performed better than the markets over the long term, but they are a small group indeed, and I have not met one of them. Nevertheless, *most investors have only a vague idea of their investment results.*

In 1997 SEC Chairman Arthur Levitt spoke to a large gathering of individual investors and asked the audience, "How many of you know precisely how you've done?" Only one third of the audience raised a

---

5. *DALBAR Special Report: Quantitative Analysis of Investor Behavior,* DALBAR Financial Services, Boston, MA, April, 1994, covering a period from 1984 through 1994, updated to 1996.

hand. If so few of these informed investors knew their actual investment results, one can only guess what a small percent of the entire investing population knows theirs.

If people do know the actual rate of return, they tend to make an educated guess. This estimate is usually much higher than the actual result. Studies show that people generally believe they are performing three to four percent higher than is the case.[6] Sometimes investors have a selective memory when it comes to total return. They only remember periods of good performance and tend to forget periods of poor performance.

Typically a person is aware of the performance of their best picks, such as a hot mutual fund or top performing stock, but the estimate degrades when their entire portfolio is taken into account. When asked to comment on long-term results, many people quote the return of their best investment as the long-term return of their entire account, even though that piece of the action may have little to do with the big picture.

We tend to alter reality to fit our perception of our abilities. Many investors for whom I have calculated results thought they were beating the markets when in fact their performance was much less. Author Peter Bernstein explains the reason for this cognitive error:[7]

> We like to believe we are above average in
> skills, intelligence, farsightedness, experience,

---

6. W. N. Goetzmann and Nadav Peles, "Cognitive Dissonance and Mutual Fund Investors," *Journal of Financial Research*, Summer 1997. Of two groups of investors, one group consisted of people who were members of an investment club, and the others were less informed participants in a small retirement plan. The informed group had no better record of guessing their performance than the uninformed group.

7. P. Bernstein, Against the Gods: The Remarkable Story of Risk, New York: John Wiley & Sons, 1996, pg. 269

refinement, and leadership. Who admits to being an incompetent driver, a feckless debater, a stupid investor, or a person with an inferior taste in clothes?

Common Errors when Calculating Investment Returns

The best way to know how a portfolio is performing is to calculate the return on a regular basis. While this exercise may seem easy, the math can get tricky. Mistakes are common and sometimes compound into very large errors. I find there are two common mistakes people make when calculating returns. Both errors are explained below.

Counting Deposits and Withdrawals as Investment Gains and Losses

A common error when calculating investment returns is to treat deposits as investment gains, and withdrawals as investment losses, rather than treating them as additions or subtractions to an account. Here is one embarrassing real-life example of a group that counted deposits as investment gain:

> The Beardstown Ladies are members of a famous investment club formed in the early 1980s. The ladies rose to prominence in the mid-1990s after the club proclaimed fantastic investments results.
>
> For ten years ending 1993, the club reported a compounded return of 23.4% in their stock portfolio versus 14.9% for the S&P 500. The ladies bought stocks of companies they knew,

like McDonald's and Coke. The investment success propelled the ladies into stardom. They appeared on TV shows, in commercials, spoke on talk radio, and, not to miss an opportunity, published best-selling books on the subject of personal finance and investing.

The world changed for the Beardstown Ladies in late 1997. A reporter from a Chicago magazine noticed something peculiar about their published investment results. After calculating the numbers several times, he concluded that a gross error had been made. The error was so large that the accounting firm of Price Waterhouse was called in to clear the air. In the final tally, the club's worst fears were realized. The ladies' actual return was only 9.1%, far below the 23.4% they reported, and well below the S&P 500.

For years the ladies deposited monthly dues into their account and classified it as an investment gain, rather than additional capital. An embarrassed treasurer blamed the error on her misunderstanding of the computer software the club was using.[8]

It is natural to make return calculation errors in a bull market. Investors expect their account to be performing well. An error may not be large enough to affect performance the short run, but if not corrected, the distortion compounds over time. Deposits and withdrawals are never treated as investment gains and losses with one exception: withdrawals used to pay direct investment expenses such as manager fees and trading

---

8. Calmetta Colman, "Beardstown Ladies Fess Up to Big Goof," Wall Street Journal, Mar 18, 1998, p. Cl.

costs are treated as a loss. This exception will be covered in more detail later in this chapter. For formulas and information on how you can calculate your return, see Appendix I, Calculating Your Investment Performance.

Buying and Selling Can Cause Errors in Calculating Investment Returns

Flip through the mutual fund section of your local newspaper, and you can quickly tell how your *funds* are performing. Although the return of the fund is listed correctly in the paper, it may not tell you much about the performance *you* have experienced in the fund. Investment returns can become distorted if you make frequent transactions in your account, like adding money each month to a 401(k) plan. The following example highlights this problem:

At the beginning of the year, suppose you invest $1,000 in a stock mutual fund, and by the end of the year, the mutual fund is up 15%. You made $150 profit. Satisfied with this result, you place another $1,000 in the mutual fund and start the second year with $2,150 invested. Unfortunately, the market moves against you and the fund falls 10%. You lost $215, leaving you with a balance of $1,935 at the end of the second year.

During that two-year period, what was the return of the *mutual fund* and what was *your* return?

The mutual fund gained 15% the first year and lost 10% the second. That's a total gain of 3.5% for the period and an annualized gain of 1.7%. Although the fund had a positive return, you did not make any money. You lost $65. That's an annualized return of minus 2.0% based on average two-year investment of $1,575 ($1,000 the first year and $2,150 the second). *The return of the mutual fund was not the same as your return. Your behavior affected your return.*

The return to the investor is not determined by the performance of the markets; it is determined by the behavior of the investor. In the example above, the fund did not cause the $65 loss. A timing error by the investor caused the loss. *This is a very important concept to understand.*

Let's look at this concept in a larger picture. The stock market returned about 18% annually over the last twenty years; however, the average investor did not experience returns anywhere close to that level of performance in their portfolios. As we will learn in Chapter 3, the average stock investor earned *significantly* less than the stock market. The timing of cash flows into and out of various investments was a large cause for the difference. As stated earlier, in order to know your exact performance, you must calculate your returns regularly and compare them to an appropriate benchmark.

Why Accurate Investment Results Are Not Provided for You

Instead of calculating the rate of return on your own, why not take the easy way out and ask your broker or financial advisor to do it for you? Good luck. Many advisors are not willing or able to produce accurate performance reports. Some advisors simply do not have the technical know-how, while others realize it may not be in their best interest to disclose performance information.

Believe it or not, most brokers and financial advisors are not trained in performance reporting techniques. The standard formulas are not covered under the stockbroker exam (Series 7), nor are they part of the Investment Advisor Exam (Series 65). Having worked in the industry for several years, I have found that advisors generally avoid discussing long-term investment performance with their clients. When someone brings up the question, the classic advisor response is, "You're doing fine."

Wrap Fee Ambiguity

Some stockbrokers and independent advisors do offer limited performance reporting services. "Wrap fee" programs typically include performance monitoring as part of the package. Wrap programs bundle several portfolio costs together into one fee, i.e. account management, commissions, custody services, and performance monitoring. The fee is typically deducted from a client's account on a quarterly basis.

I find the performance reports of most wrap fee programs to be confusing and ambiguous. The reports tend to highlight an account's *gross* return rather than its *net* return. This means the fee paid for the service is *added back* to the account before a return is calculated. This obviously overstates the results. Assume you open a wrap fee account in January for $100,000 and agree to pay a 3,0% fee. During the year securities are bought and sold, and $3,000 in fees deducted. By the end of December the account value is $98,000. A logical person would calculate a 2.0% loss for the account, but most wrap fee reports show a gain of 1.0%. Why the difference? Most wrap fee programs do not consider fees as an expense. They are counted as a *withdrawal* from the account. As a result, the 1.0% gain is highlighted on the report.

Hogwash! Unfair! Reporting gross returns to individual investors is a deceptive and unethical practice, although standard at most brokerage firms. Although the SEC does require disclosure of *net-of-fee* performance, many firms place that number near the end of the performance report in an obscure and ambiguous location. In my opinion, this is done because the advisor has failed to achieve the investment objective, and he is trying to hide the true return. As an aside, many advisors use marketing material highlighting performance that excludes fees and expenses. Although advisors are obligated to show a prospective client their net results, they often forget to point to the fine print.

Performance reports printed for individual investors should be easy to understand and net of all fees. The performance should also be compared to an *appropriate* market benchmark. Many advisors choose a benchmark that makes them look good, rather than comparing the results to an appropriate index. I once met an advisor who tried to compare his high-yield junk bond portfolio to Treasury bills! Until the SEC cracks down on performance reporting, you should look hard at the reports you get from your advisor. The best protection is to run the numbers yourself and compare the performance to an appropriate market index.

Chapter 3

Measuring the Performance Gap

*One of the great differences between a wise man and a
fool: the former only wishes for what he may possibly
obtain, the latter desires impossibilities.*

—Democritus

Over the last two decades, the stock and bond markets
have delivered superior returns, better than over any
other twenty-year period in the history of Wall Street.
Most individual investors in those markets assumed
they were capturing their fair share of those gains, but in
reality, the average investor experienced performance
well below the return of the markets. While this is a
somber fact, it is not a new phenomenon. Individual
investors have a long history of below-average performance that spans the twentieth century.

A History of Underachievement

In the early 1900s a man who called himself Don Guyon
worked at a prominent Wall Street brokerage firm. In
1915, after years of observing clients buying and selling
securities in the financial markets, he decided to conduct
a study to see if he could improve their trading skill[9].
Guyon began documenting the trades of six clients,
meticulously recording all their trades in five active

stocks. This was no easy task. Back in the days before computers, all transactions were recorded by hand. To accurately assess the investment skill of each client, Guyon needed to match all the sell orders against all the buy orders. He also had to adjust for stock splits and dividend payments. The profit or loss of each trade was recorded in a cumulative balance.

Guyon diligently tracked this activity for eight months. When he thought he had enough data, he tallied the results. During the period, the average gain of the five stocks was 65%, with each one returning from 29% to 129%. The investors themselves thought they had done fairly well during the period, but the numbers were quite the opposite. While the average stock gained during the period, the average client *lost* 3.5%.

How did the clients lose money while the stocks surged ahead? Guyon theorized the problem was not the stocks but *the behavior of investors buying and selling the stocks*. Generally, the clients waited for a stock to rise in value before committing a large amount of money to it. Apparently they felt more comfortable buying stocks that had recently gone up. If a stock went down after purchase it was sold at a loss. This trend-following behavior caused excessive portfolio turnover. Many trades were profitable, but after adjusting for trading costs, all the profit disappeared. Based on this new information, Guyon recommended that his clients hold their positions longer and avoid the cost of trading.

This early study showed how investor behavior can affect portfolio returns, and that those returns can be far different from the returns of the markets.

---

9. Don Guyan, *One-Way Pockets*, Fraser Publishing Company, Burlington Vermont, 1965. Originally published by Capstone Publishing Company, NY, 1917. The five stocks studied were US Steel, Crucible Steel, Baldwin Locomotive, Studebaker Corporation, and Westinghouse Electric.

Times Have Not Changed

Have investment results and trading habits improved from the early 1900s now that we have superior information at our fingertips? Recently, one independent research company attempted to answer that question. In 1995, Boston-based DALBAR Financial Services published an in-depth study of *investors'* performance in mutual funds. The purpose of the study was to see how much money investors made in mutual funds, as opposed to how well the mutual funds performed in relation to the markets. They originally studied mutual fund investors from 1984 through 1994, then updated the information in 1995 and 1996.

DALBAR divided the mutual fund universe into stock and bond funds and further divided the funds based on the distribution method (load funds sold by brokers and no-load funds sold directly). These categories allowed DALBAR to study the behavior of investors in different markets.[10]

Mutual funds measure return based on relative performance to a market, whereas investors measure return based on the *dollars* they gained or lost. Similar to the Guyon study, DALBAR tallied the profit or loss on each mutual fund traded during the period and calculated a cumulative total dollar gain for all fund investors over the years. DALBAR measured the difference between the dollar gains of investors and the reported returns of mutual funds. The results are hard to believe at first reading.

---

10. DALBAR Financial Services, Boston, MA, excerpts taken from the DALBAR Special Report, Quantitative Analysis of Investor Behavior, June 1996. A considerable amount of data and text in this section were taken directly from the DALBAR study. The DALBAR report is available to the public on request.

DALBAR Results From 1984
Through 1996

Researchers found a large gap between the average reported return of the funds and actual investor profits in those funds. It did not matter whether the fund category was direct market no-load funds or broker-sold load funds, the *performance gap* for both categories was extremely large. The gap between reported mutual fund returns and investor returns is illustrated below:

Gap Between Fund and Investor Returns

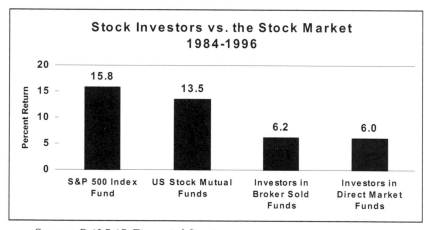

Source: DALBAR Financial Services

The average stock mutual fund achieved a 13.5% return during the period. However, mutual fund investors did not achieve anything close to the return of the average fund. Average investors saw their capital compound at only 6.1% annually during the 13-year period. In addition, an S&P 500 Index fund achieved a 15.8% annual return over the period, outperforming everything. This huge performance gap was created by a variety of factors to be discussed in later chapters.

Notice the 0.2% difference in returns between broker-sold funds and direct market funds. The data suggest that investors who purchased commission funds achieved higher returns than did no-load investors. DALBAR determined that investors who bought load funds held onto their positions longer and thus had an increase in total performance. However, the study did not take into account commissions paid to buy broker-sold funds. Thus, load fund returns were lower than those stated in the study. While the issue of load versus no-load is a hotly debated topic in the investment industry, the fact remains that investors in *both* categories did poorly.

Performance of Bond Fund Investors

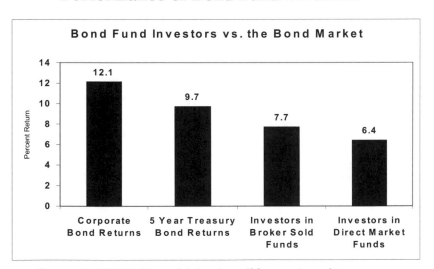

Source: DALBAR Financial Services, Ibbotson Associates

Bond fund investors also experienced a performance gap. The return of investors in bond funds is compared to the return of a five-year Treasury note and a corporate bond composite over the same period. Both indexes were reduced by 0.20% to reflect the cost of buying the bonds. Overall bond fund investors performed more than 2.0% below the five-year Treasury note and 5.0% less that corporate bonds. Investors in broker-sold funds investors achieved a higher return than direct market investing direct market investors; however, this was before the commission charge. If the data were adjusted for sales loads, it is debatable whether load fund investors would have made more money than no-load fund investors did. In either case, all investors made less money than they would have made had they simply purchased individual Treasury notes or corporate bonds.

What does the DALBAR study tell us? It makes it clear that the average individual investor does not come close to the returns of the markets they invest in. It is also clear that investment return is far more dependent on investor behavior than on market returns. Despite all the "buy and hold" literature disseminated by the investment industry, the public is still very much inclined toward trading in and out of various investments at precisely the wrong time.

The study also provides little evidence that stockbrokers and other financial advisors effectively manage their clients' money. Based on the high correlation of returns between broker-sold funds and direct market funds, one can only conclude that investors do not gain monetarily by seeking the advice of investment "experts," especially after factoring in commissions and fees.

Other Recent Studies of Investor Performance

The DALBAR results sparked other research into the area of investor returns. Morningstar conducted a study of growth fund investors in 1995. It was limited to US growth funds and covered a five-year period from June 1989 through May 1994. The conclusion of the study was consistent with the DALBAR results. The average growth fund in the category returned 12.5% during the period whereas the average investor in growth funds lost 2.2% of their capital. The Morningstar study is important because it highlights the damage that can result from chasing hot performing funds. We will take a closer look at this study in Chapter 5, "Chasing the Hot Dot."

Money magazine published an informative article on investor returns in April 1997. The article highlighted mutual funds that achieved high returns during the previous year but lost investors' money during the same time.[11] For example, *Money* looked at the Van Wagoner Emerging Growth fund (VWEG). During the first half of 1996, VWEG shot up over 60%. An investor who put $10,000 in the fund on January 1 would have had $16,000 by the end of June. Unfortunately, few people put money in the fund in January. Assets were less than $1 million.

The superior performance of VWEG in the first half of '96 caught the eye of investors. Assets exploded to over $800 million by the end of July, but it was too late. During the second half of the year, the fund collapsed. VWEG fell over 30%, from its peak, ending at 27% for the year. While this is a great return for the entire year, most investors caught only the 30% downturn in the second half. *Money* calculated the average shareholder loss at 20% of their investment, for a total of $100 million. Even though VWEG beat the stock market in 1996, the average investor in the fund lost money. Published performance can be vastly different from the experience of investors.

The SEC is Aware and Concerned

The Securities and Exchange Commission (SEC) is fully aware of the discrepancies between market returns and investor returns. Barry Barbash, director of

---

11. Jason Zweig, "Funds That Really Make Money For Their Investors," Money, April 1997, pg. 124-134

the SEC Investment Management Division, would like to see changes in the way performance is reported to clients. During a speech given to the Investment Company Institute in March 1997, Mr. Barbash said he would like to see personalized performance data on mutual fund statements that shows how an investor's buying and selling affected their results. "The discrepancy between a fund's performance and that of its shareholders can be large," he said. "Investors would benefit from knowing how well they did as opposed to how well their fund did."

Barbash acknowledged that the cost of this data would add an expense to owning the fund, and educating the shareholders would be a challenge. Recently, a handful of investment companies have decided to offer this information to their clients on an annual basis.

How Stock Pickers Have Fared

Mutual funds have become vehicle of choice for stock market investors, but there are still a number of do-it-yourself stock pickers around. Have trading habits improved since the days of Don Guyon? Not according to Terrance Odean of the University of California. In 1997, Odean conducted a landmark study of 10,000 individual accounts at a large discount brokerage firm. He analyzed the performance of 97,483 stock trades in those accounts between 1988 and 1993. Odean kept track of the stocks each investor sold and compared them to the performance of the ones they bought.[12]

Odean compared the results over several time periods. During the two year period, the stocks sold beat the market by 2.9% and the stocks bought underperformed

---

12. As reported in Registered Representative magazine, July 1997, pg. 38

by 0.7%. Transaction costs reduced returns by another 5.9%. Odean figured the average stock investor lost 9.5% in value trading stocks during the period. In all time frames, the stock traders lost value over buy-and-hold investors.

"Overconfidence is a big issue here," Odean states. Investors appear to think they're better stock pickers than they actually are. He found several examples of a herding mentality. Although over 10,000 stocks are actively traded on the US exchanges, a majority of the accounts held the same fad stocks. Most of those stocks were recent Wall Street darlings that had made a large price gain in the past twelve months.

Robert Shiller, professor of economics at Yale University, found similar herding patterns in his research. Shiller surveyed individual investors and found that "interpersonal communication" was the number one factor affecting an investment decision. Investors buy what their friends are buying and sell what their friends are selling.[13]

Dr. Jeremy Siegal of the Wharton School attempted to quantify the results of individual stock pickers. In his book, *Stocks for the Long Run*, Siegal suggests that average stock investor lags the market by about 5.0% per year.[14] He states the reason for this shortfall is a lack of information and skill. In order to achieve superior returns, Siegal believes you must posses superior information and have the skill to use it. Since few individual investors fall into this category, most perform poorly. Even professional money mangers have only average information and average skill, so they do not beat the markets, either.

---

13. Robert Shiller, Market Volatility, MIT Press, Cambridge, MA, 1992
14. Jeremy J. Siegal, Stocks for the Long Run, Irwin Press, 1994, pg. 292.

Having spent many years monitoring the performance of individual investors, I can attest to the accuracy of the above studies. I have yet to meet a non-professional investor who *consistently* achieves superior returns. There are times when people guess right, but over the long haul, the markets are far more efficient than the average investor. Playing the market can be fun, and it is a great hobby. Unfortunately, many people confuse luck with skill, and eventually wreak havoc on their retirement savings.

A Closer Look at the Performance Gap

In the last two chapters we learned that most individual investors achieve returns significantly below the markets they invest in, yet they believe they are faring much better. Appendix I provides the formulas needed to calculate individual returns and help identify a problem. The difference between the markets' return and investors' return is called the *performance gap*. The next three chapters look at three reasons why the gap exists.

Chapter 4

The High Cost of Low Returns

A billion dollars here, a billion dollars there, and pretty soon you're talking about real money.

–Everett Dirksen

Our examination of the performance gap begins with the obvious, a discussion of fees and expenses. As a general rule, investment costs detract from performance on a one-for-one basis. There is no advantage to paying a high price for investment products and advice. The perception that superior returns can be achieved by paying a large fee to an advisor is a marketing myth. No data exist to support such wishful thinking. If you spend a lot of money seeking superior returns, you will only end up further behind.

The average investor faces a mountain of expenses, many of which they don't even know about. Brokerage commissions, management fees, custodial costs, and sales loads are just the tip of the iceberg; the most damaging costs can be hidden below the surface. Hidden from investors are trading spreads, market impact, opportunity costs, soft dollar expenses, taxes, and other expenses that degrade returns. Taking all costs except taxes into consideration, the average individual investor gives up about 3.0% per year on their stock funds and about 1.5% per year on their bond funds. If you hire a financial advisor to pick investments for you, subtract *another* 1.0% or so from returns. Except for the very fortunate, investment costs prohibit individual investors from achieving long-term results close to those of the markets they invest in, let alone beat them.

The True Cost of Investing in Stocks and Bonds

The best way to understand investment costs is to analyze a basic stock and bond trade. Stocks and bonds are the building blocks of most investment portfolios, and the cost of trading these securities are inherent in all products including mutual funds, unit trusts, and wrap fee accounts. One important cost that is often overlooked is the cost of *taxation*. Paying unnecessary tax for investment gain can cause a large reduction in long-term wealth. Tax considerations are mentioned briefly in this chapter and are covered in detail in Chapter 15. Wise investors work hard to reduce the cost of investing, and this is the first step toward reducing the performance gap.

The Cost of Executing a Stock Trade

Executing a stock trade is more expensive than most people think. Besides the obvious commission, returns are often adversely affected by the bid/ask trading spread, the market impact of the trade, and the opportunity cost. All investors incur some form of commission cost, even large institutional investors. Only SEC licensed brokers are allowed to trade securities on the major exchanges, and they charge a fee for their service.

The commission paid on a stock trade varies depending on the broker and brokerage firm. If you sell a thousand shares of General Motors, the commission may be $800 through a full-service broker, but only $7 though a Internet broker. Does the $800 full service brokerage firm do anything different from what the $7 broker does? Not really. Both trades are routed through an electronic trading system and clear through the same channels. As a result, the price per share you receive is typically the same regardless of the broker. Unless you are trading thousands of shares at a time or trading an obscure over-the-counter stock, the difference between a full service broker and a discount broker is negligible.

The stock market is a live auction, and professional traders run the auction. They *bid* for stock when investors want to sell and *offer* stock when someone wants to buy. The difference between the bid and the offer price is known as the bid/ask spread. The spread varies widely firm stock to stock, depending in part on the liquidity of the stock. Large companies with many shares outstanding usually trade with a small spread, perhaps six cents per share. Small companies with few shares outstanding can trade with a large spread, perhaps one dollar per share or more. Many stock investors find the cost of the bid/ask spread is much more expensive than the commissions they pay.

Hidden Costs of Trading Stocks

The cost of stock trading is not limited to the commission and bid/ask spread. There are abstract expenses as well. One cost is the market's reaction to a buy or sell order. It is a new experience for novice investors to learn that their buying and selling can change the market price of a stock. Consider this old Wall Street story:

One day an old wise investor passed a stock tip to an eager young man. The young man knew this was a good tip, so he called a broker and bought a thousand shares of the stock for two dollars per share. The next day the stock was quoted at three dollars, and in his joy the man bought another thousand shares. By the third day the stock was offered at five dollars. The young man could not believe his good fortune, and he borrowed $5,000 against his house to buy a thousand more shares. By the fourth day the stock was offered at eight dollars. Sitting on a sizable profit, the young man told his broker to SELL IT ALL, to which the broker laughed and said, "To whom would you like me to sell? Only three thousand shares have traded all week!"

Most individual investors never consider the impact their trades have on the market, but large mutual fund mangers are keenly aware of the problem. Consider the difficulty encountered in selling hundreds of thousands of shares of a thinly traded stock. It can take several days or even weeks to trade the position. John Bogle Jr. studied the market impact of trading small-cap stocks in a mutual fund. He found that small-cap funds with assets over $350 million begin to suffer a significant deterioration in performance due to the market impact of trading. Small-cap mutual funds with over $700 million generally lose more money to market impact than the manager could possibly gain with superior stock selections.[15] The market impact of trading can be costly to investors, but you will not find this expense listed in any mutual fund prospectus.

Opportunity cost is even more abstract than market impact. Generally, it takes time for money managers to process a trade even if it is a very liquid stock. Opportunity cost is the price change that occurs between the time a manager decides to trade a stock and the time it is actually executed on the trading desk. If a fund manager has information on a stock that has not been widely disseminated, he must execute trades quickly. It will only be a matter of seconds before the information is widely

---

15. John Bogle Jr, CFA, Optimal Fund Size and Maximizing Returns, Investing in Small-Cap and Microcap Securities, AIMR Seminar, September 25, 1996, Boston MA

known and fully reflected in stock price. In a fast paced market, time is money. The slower the trades are executed, the greater the opportunity cost.

If you have ever taken a trip on a cruise ship you will understand the concept of hidden costs. An advertisement in the newspaper may read, "For only $695 per person, you can enjoy an all-inclusive week on a beautiful luxury liner." Sounds like a bargain, but that's not the end of the story. In order to get to the ship, you must fly to Miami, which could cost at least $300 round trip. Parking at the airport costs $70 per week. Once you are on board, you discover all sightseeing trips ashore are extra, and they are not cheap. Add $150 for a couple of land tours. Like an occasional fruit drink while cruising? They will cost you $5 each. At the end of the trip, don't forget to add up your tips to the waiters, busboys, and room service. That runs another $250. By the end of the week, your $695 vacation costs $1,500. The hidden cost of the trip can be more damaging than the advertised cost. Investing in the markets is no different.

The Cost of a Bond Trade

Bond trading involves the same costs as stock trading, but the brokerage commission is typically built into the price of the bond. Most trades are conducted over the counter, meaning the brokerage firm with whom you are dealing will likely sell you bonds they have in their own inventory. The difference between the sales price of a bond and the buy price it is known as the sales spread. Since each broker is independent, sale spreads vary, and it pays to shop around for the best price.

To give you an example of a bond trade, assume you want to sell a bond that has a current market value of $10,000. You call your broker to request a bid. The broker will show the bond to the firm's bond trader and come back to you with a bid price. For this example the bid is $9,700. If you accept this bid, the broker buys the bonds from you and turns it over to the trader. The trader puts the bond in the firm's inventory and then re-offers it to clients for $10,000. When the bond is sold to another client, the firm realizes a profit of $300, of which your broker received a portion. The National Association of Securities Dealers (NASD) has rules that govern the spreads on bond trades, and excessive spreads are illegal. More information on trading bonds can be found in Part III, Chapter 13, Investing in the Bond Market.

Mutual Fund Fees and Expenses

Now that we understand the basics of stock and bond trading, it is time to add two other layers of expense. Mutual funds and private portfolio managers charge management fees to run portfolios. With a mutual fund, this fee is listed in the prospectus as part of the *expense* ratio. If you work with a stockbroker or other financial advisor, there is an extra commission or fee included. This section explains the expenses inherent in commission mutual funds and wrap fee accounts.

Mutual Fund Expenses

Open any mutual fund prospectus and you find a section titled Portfolio Expenses or similar wording. This is a listing of the fees charged directly to the mutual fund on an annual basis. They include investment manager fees, marketing fees, legal costs, administrative fees, and miscellaneous expenses. Several fund families charge a 12b-1 fee. This annual charge is paid to brokers and other advisors who have investors in the fund. [needs more explanation. What is it? What is the rationale?] Fees for 12b-1 provide no benefit to current shareholders and are a hot topic of discussion between the SEC and the investment industry.

The *Operating Expense Ratio* is found by dividing all these fees by the total amount of money in the fund. A typical operating expense ratio runs about 1.5% for stock funds and 1.0% for bond funds, however, ratios can vary widely from fund to fund. Recently there have been a number of highly publicized studies suggesting mutual fund fees are dropping. That is a misconception. If you eliminate low-cost producers Vanguard and Fidelity from the universe of fund companies, fees have actually crept higher over the years.[16]

Studies show that high fees are not good for investors. Table 1 compares the returns of high expense growth and income funds to low expense funds over a ten- and fifteen-year period. The evidence makes a strong case for investing low fee funds.

Table 1: Growth and Income Funds Expense Ratio Verses Performance 1984 - 1998

Category	Expense Ratio	10-Year Return	15-Year Return
All 65 Funds	1.27%	15.6%	14.6%
Low Fee	0.69%	16.5%	15.7%
High Fee	1.83%	14.8%	13.8%

Source: Morningstar Principia

Trading Costs within Funds

The cost of trading stocks and bonds within a fund are not included in the expense ratio, but they do add to the

---

16. Scott Cooley, Revising Fund Costs: Up or Down, Morningstar Mutual Funds, February 21, 1999

expense of managing a fund. As explained earlier, mutual fund managers must pay commissions and bid/ ask spreads when they trade securities. The more trades a manager makes during the year, the more she reduces the value of the fund.

Table 2 compares the returns of high turnover Growth and Income funds to low turnover funds. The data clearly suggest that portfolio turnover is one of the factors driving returns.

Table 2: Growth and Income Funds Portfolio Turnover Versus Performance 1984 - 1998

Category	1998 Turnover Rate	10-Year Return	15-Year Return
All 65 Funds	68%	15.6%	14.6%
Low Turn-over	24%	16.5%	15.5%
High Turn-over	109%	14.8%	13.8%

Source: Morningstar Principia

According to Morningstar, the average turnover rate of a US equity fund is about 80% per year, meaning that about four out of five stocks are held less than twelve months. This turnover generates a brokerage commission cost of about 0.30% per year.[17] Some funds have higher turnover, which increases the commission cost of those funds. On average, small-cap portfolios have about twice the turnover of large-cap funds.

---

17. Miles Livingston and Edward S. O'Neal, Mutual Fund Brokerage Commissions, *Journal of Financial Research*, Vol. 19, no. 2 (Summer 1996): 273-92

In addition to the commission expense, mutual funds sometimes incur a profound market impact cost. Plexas Group is a research and consulting firm that tracks trading costs for investment companies. Plexas estimates the market impact of a large-cap US equity funds run about 0.40% per year and small-cap funds were significantly higher with a market impact about 1.50%.[18]

One final hidden expense faced by almost all mutual funds is the cost of holding cash in a portfolio. Cash includes Treasury bills and other short-term interest bearing investments. Most stock mutual funds hold between 5.0% and 10% in cash, depending on market conditions. Over time, the cash portion of a portfolio reduces the return of the fund. For example, if the stock market went up by 10%, and a stock mutual fund held 5.0% in cash paying 4.0%, the *cash drag* of the fund was 0.30% for the year (5.0% of the portfolio under-performed the stock market by 6.0%). The cash portion of a stock fund is charged the same management fee as the stock portion, making it a very expensive money market fund. Market impact and cash drag are *not* part of the *Operating Expense Ratio,* but they do reduce shareholder value.

Charles Ellis wrote in 1972 that the reason professional managers cannot beat the market is that they have effectively become the market.[19] Commissions, fees, and hidden expenses have precluded mutual funds from achieving market returns over the past twenty-five years, and I do not anticipate a change over the next twenty-five.

---

18. Plexas Group, Quality of Trade Execution in Comparative Perspective: AMEX vs. NYSE vs. NASDAQ, August 1996, Plexas Group Inc., Los Angeles, CA
19. Charles D. Ellis, *Investment Policy; How to Win the Loser's Game,* Business One Irwin, NY, Page 5

Sales Charges

The final cost is the cost of advice. Stockbrokers, insurance agents, and other financial advisors sell over 60% of all mutual funds. Typically these funds carry some sort of sales commission or fee that goes to the salesperson. Until a few years ago, most investors paid a sales commission to buy mutual funds. This commission is called a "load" and was historically paid up front. Times have changed. The fund industry now offers all kinds of ways to pay your advisor. There are "A" share front-end loads, "B" share back-end loads, "C" share level loads, "L" share combined loads, and "Z" shares for use in wrap fee programs.

A large bulk of fund sales is through brokerage firms, but this method of distribution does not come cheap. Many funds are required to pay *access charges* to get in the door of a brokerage firm. A fund company may spend $100,000 or more per year for the right to talk to brokers at a well-known firm. Then they must spend more money wining and dining the brokers to make them listen. In many cases, the level of access a fund company has within a brokerage firm depends on the size of the check its representative writes. At some brokerage firms, the highest paying fund companies earn special privileges such as the right to be on the "recommended fund list." *Pay to play* is a big revenue source for brokerage firm and a necessary evil for most mutual fund companies. As David J. Evens of Glencoe Investments says, "Performance is nice; but marketing is better."[20]

Wrap-Fee Services

In the 1970s E. F. Hutton developed a private managed account program for individual investors with assets of $100,000 or more. The program allowed small investors

---

20. Article by Jim McTague, Dropouts, *Barron's,* April 7, 1997

to hire institutional money managers who normally invest for large clients. Clients paid for the service under an all-inclusive "wrap fee." The fee includes commissions, manager fees, custody, monitoring, and other miscellaneous charges and can run as high as 3.0% per year.

Hutton's wrap fee program was an instant success and was quickly copied by other brokerage firms. Over time, the wrap concept spilled over into the mutual fund industry. Financial advisors began charging annual fees to build and manage mutual fund portfolios. The popularity of all wrap fee programs has mushroomed. Over one trillion dollars are now under "wrap," according to a 1998 study by Charles Schwab Inc.

The Hidden Costs in Wrap Fee Accounts

Large brokerage houses are the biggest sellers of wrap fee products, although banks, insurance companies, independent advisors, and even accountants are now offering the wrap service. The cost of a wrap fee account can be as high as 3.0% per year for a stock account, although the going rate seems closer to 2.0%.

The wrap fee is supposed to cover all trading costs and management fees. But it doesn't. The fee does NOT include costs such as the bid/ask spread, market impact, or opportunity cost of trading. These unreported expenses can run an additional 1.0% per year depending on the style of the account. In addition, the wrap fee is charged on cash sitting in the portfolio, which creates the most expensive money market fund you will ever own. For example, assume you pay 2.0% for a wrap account and the manager places 90.0% of your money in stocks and leaves 10% in the money market fund. You are charged the same 2.0% fee on the money sitting in the money fund as you are on the stock portion. In addition, money market funds have their own internal cost of about 0.6%, bringing your total expense on the 10% in the money market fund to 2.6%!

Asset growth can be a major problem of investment companies in large wrap programs, and that adds to your cost. Most money management firms are admitted to large wrap fee programs *after* they finished a period of superior performance. Unfortunately, the success of a manager often leads to their failure. As brokers and other advisors throw new money at these firms, many develop operational problems. They can no longer manage money the same way they did in the past. These realities usually cause a significant deterioration in returns, and the eventual downfall of the manager. I have watched this boom-bust cycle occur dozens of times with new managers in wrap fee programs.

Mutual Fund Wrap Programs

In the late 1980s discount broker Charles Schwab introduced the concept of a mutual fund supermarket. Clients could buy and sell no-load mutual funds from hundreds of different fund families all under one roof. As a result, financial advisors began to offer trading strategies through the Schwab OneSource® program. Advisors charged their clients a fee to pick "superior" mutual funds or time the market. The wrap-a-fund concept was so popular that now every major brokerage house and insurance company has such a program.

A mutual fund wrap program is actually a *fee within a fee* within a fee. First, there are stock and bond trading costs internal to the mutual funds. Second, each internal fund charges management fees and operating expenses. Third, the financial advisor charges an extra fee to pick funds for you. After accounting for all fees, hidden or otherwise, investors in mutual fund wrap program can pay upwards of 5.0% per year to have their funds managed. There is no chance an advisor will overcome those costs and achieve market results.

Other Packaged Products

It is always thus, impelled by a state of mind which is destined not to last, that we make our most irrevocable decisions.

—Marcel Proust

Investment products are packaged and repackaged in a variety of ways. The marketing of these products has changed over the years, but the products themselves have remained fairly consistent. The list of packaged products is long, and it grows each day. There are unit investment trusts, limited partnerships, commodity funds, variable annuities, variable life, and the list goes on. If there is a common thread among all packaged products, it is that they are very expensive and typically charge high commissions.

The high commission drives the sale of packaged products. Some advisor will find something good to say about any product if the *yield to broker* is large enough,. Many insurance products pay the seller 6.0% or more up front, followed by the annual trailer. Some commodity funds charge investors 10% or more *per year.* At the 1996 annual meeting of Berkshire Hathaway, Warren Buffett labeled a unit investment trust a "high commission product with substantial annual fees." Commissions, not the investors need, drive the sale of packaged products.

Summary

The more you pay for investment products and advice, the less you make on your investment portfolio. About 3.0% of the performance gap is a direct result of investment costs before accounting for commissions. The best place to begin to reduce the performance gap is to seek out low-cost investments that have no commissions attached. Several alternatives to commission-weighted fees are covered in Part III of this book.

Chapter 5

Market Timing Myths

One of the funny things about the stock market, every time one man is buying, another is selling, and both think they are astute.

—William Feather

The search for superior investment returns leads many people to speculate on the future direction of the markets. Those who can foretell the future can make spectacular profits. *Market timing* is the common name used to describe this strategy, although it is also called *tactical asset allocation.*

Can tomorrow's prices be determined with today's information? Identifying market moves before they occur has challenged mankind for thousands of years. So far, no one has found a crystal ball that consistently works, though many have claimed they have. In today's financial markets it is difficult if not impossible for one person to know more than the next, and superior market timing implies superior information. Unless you have superior information *and* can interpret that information quickly, there is little use in timing the markets to try to increase returns on your investment. Markets adjust too fast to allow time for a meaningful response by institutional investors as well as by individuals.

Although there is little chance to make excess profits by market timing, many people believe in the concept and spend a great deal of time and money searching for an ideal strategy. Wall Street and the financial press cater to this need by selling all sorts of market timing services. There are market valuation models, charting services, guru call-in numbers, newsletters, web sites, fax services, and a variety of gimmicks designed to separate investors from their money. Unfortunately, there is little academic evidence that any of this works. The vast majority of people who follow these strategies experience returns well below the market they are trying to beat, with no reduction in risk.

This chapter highlights the portion of the performance gap related to market timing. We will review the performance of various timing strategies as well as the results of popular "experts." Understanding the shortfall of market timing is a crucial step to understanding the performance gap. Bold market predictions by popular gurus occasionally cause a short-term price reaction, but there is little follow-through. Investors are wise to save their money, ignore the hype, and focus on long-term goals.

Academic Research on Timing the Market

Read almost any college textbook on investing and you will find a section on market timing. There will likely be a paragraph or two describing market timing, and then a host of research explaining why it does not work. Researchers involved in almost every major study of market timing, including those conducted by Nobel Laureate economists, have concluded that any attempt to profit by predicting the direction of the market will ultimately fail.

This decade is strewn with examples of bright people who thought they built a better mousetrap that could consistently extract abnormal returns from financial markets. Some succeed for a time. But while there may occasionally be misconfigurations among market prices that allow abnormal returns, they do not persist.
—Federal Reserve Chairman Alan Greenspan

Any timing system designed to extract excessive returns from the market will eventually fail. If a strategy was developed that did work, it would be a closely guarded secret and would only benefit a few people for a short period of time. When others figure out the strategy, excess profits would quickly fade. Market timing strategies sold to the public *en masse* may have worked in the past, but they have no chance for excess profits in the future. The life has been taken out of them a long time ago.

In the early 1900s, Harry Houdini exposed widespread fraud in the fortune-telling industry. Houdini offered a large reward to anyone who could prove they could speak to the dead. Though many soothsayers tried to fool Houdini, he uncovered all their tricks. No one ever collected the prize. Today, market timers run similar businesses. The skill is not in telling the future but in persuading people they have the ability to tell the future. It doesn't matter if an advisor can predict the market; what's important to the advisor is *marketing the prediction.* Selling advice is much more profitable than following it.

A Short History of Market Timers

If I have noticed anything over these 60 years on Wall Street, it is that people do not succeed in forecasting what's going to happen to the stock market.
—Benjamin Graham

Wall Street gurus have been predicting market prices since shares began trading in the 1800s, and researchers tracking those predictions have found no value in them. Alfred Cowles, a research analyst and statistician, studied Wall Street forecasts early in the century. In 1933 he reported his findings in the prestigious Econometric Journal. Cowles statistically proved there was no benefit to market forecasts published by Wall Street strategists. John Maynard Keynes, a famous economist and highly successful stock investor rendered the same conclusion:

The idea of wholesale shifts is for various reasons impractical and indeed undesirable. Most of those who attempt it sell too late and buy too late, and do both too often, incurring heavy expenses and developing too unsettled and speculative state of mind.

Stock market timing strategies have evolved over the years. Until the 1960s, the rule of thumb was to sell when the dividend yield on stocks fell below interest rates on bonds, and buy when the opposite occurred. However, in 1959 stock yields fell below bond yields and never looked back. During the 1960s the dividend strategy was revised and new approach was established. When the market yield fell below 3.0% wise investors were supposed to sell and when it rose above 5.0% investors should buy. That idea failed in the 1990s when the dividend dropped below 1.5%. Investors who followed popular dividend strategies missed one of the greatest bull markets in history.

Market timing beliefs always fight the last war. Timing techniques designed during the rising inflationary period from the 1940s through early 1980s did not work during the disinflation period of the late 1980s and 1990s. Peter Lynch, former manager of the Fidelity Magellan Fund, commented about the failure of market timers throughout the twentieth century:

The investment geniuses among us could have put all their money into the S&P 500 stocks in the 1920s, switched to long-term corporate bonds in the 1930s, moved to into small-company stocks in the 1940s, back into the S&P 500 in the 1950s, back to small stocks in the 1960s and the 1970s, and returned to the S&P 500 in the 1980s. The people who followed that inspired strategy are now billionaires living on the coast of France. Since I never met a single billionaire who made his or her fortune exactly in this fashion, I must assume that they are in short supply relative to the rest of us who exhibit normal intelligence.[21]

Wall Street and Market Timing Models

Many sellers of investment advice feel the term *market timing* has limited appeal. It almost sounds cheap. Therefore, Wall Street came up with a new name called *tactical asset allocation*. Many people claim there is a difference, but don't be misled by that argument. Tactical asset allocation is based on the belief that the markets are predictable, and that it is possible to profit by moving money from one market to another at an appropriate time. In other words, it is market timing.

Wall Street pumps out mountains of asset allocation information on a regular basis. Brokerage firms recommend tactical weightings in stocks, bonds, and cash as part of their regular research routine. A typical allocation may be 55% in stocks, 40% in bonds, and 5.0% in money funds. The allocation will change on regular basis according to "market conditions." When a company changes its asset allocation they do so with

---

21. Peter Lynch, *Beating the Street,* Simon & Schuster, New York, 1993, pg. 17

great fanfare and lots media coverage. They try to make it a marketing extravaganza.

Does tactical asset allocation really work, or is Wall Street taking Main Street for a ride? Look no further than *The Wall Street Journal*'s running scorecard on the issue. The results of tactical asset allocation models recommended by the major brokerage firms are regularly published in the *Journal*. The return of the models are ranked against each other and compared to the results of a static allocation. The static "Robot" blend holds 55% stock, 35% bonds, and 10% in money market funds. Although the robot blend never changes, the brokerage firms are free to vary their allocation anytime.[22]

A 10% money market position in the Robot blend should have made this model easy to beat, but that is not the case. The average brokerage firm does not beat the Robot portfolio. For five years ending in 1998, eight out of twelve firms were below the static blend with two of the largest brokerage firms falling significantly below the benchmark.[23] Of the firms who outmaneuvered the markets, no firm held the top spot for the entire period. One important point about the *Journal's* study is that it suffers from *survivorship bias.* Several firms have dropped out of the study over the years due to mergers, acquisitions, or their own request. As a result, only the performance of surviving firms are reflected in the study, which pushed the average higher.

---

22. John Dorfman, "Experts Urge Cutting Exposure to Stocks," *The Wall Street Journal,* August 11, 1997, C1
23. Aaron Lucchetti, "Strategist Post Worst Results in 8 Years", *The Wall Street Journal,* October 28, 1998, pg C1

The Real Reason for Tactical Asset Allocations

There is no denying that the more financial predictions you make the more business you do and the more commissions you get.
—Fred Schwed, Jr., "Where Are the Customers' Yachts?"

If market timing does not work, why do so many brokerage firms spend time and money trying to make it work? The answer has nothing to do with finding a formula to beat the markets. Instead, it has to do with generating commissions and marketing the firm. When clients hear their broker has made an asset allocation change they become curious. This leads to phone conversations, which leads to more business. It is a known fact that brokerage firms increase sales after they change their opinion on the markets. An internal study by one large brokerage firm found sales in its wrap fee mutual fund products increased *substantially* following a suggested asset allocation change. Ironically, an informal study of those changes reveals that clients would have been better off ignoring the advice. The recommendations led to *lower* return overall.

Investment Newsletters and Market Predictions

There's an old joke about high school physical education teachers that goes like this: Those who cannot do— teach. Those who cannot teach—teach phys ed. The same logic can be applied to market timers who sell investment newsletters. Those who do not understand the market time the market. Those who cannot time the market sell market timing newsletters.

Look through any issue of *Investors Business Daily* and you will find dozens of ads for newsletters claiming superior market timing ability. John Graham and Campbell Harvey of Duke University graded the ability of newsletters to time the market and found little evidence to support the marketing claims.[24] The study covered hundreds of newsletters published between 1983 and 1995. Following market timing advice of the letter writers would have produced only a 12% return for the period, while the S&P 500 compounded at a 17% return. An abstract of the results is as follows:

> Many investment newsletters offer market-timing advice; that is, they are supposed to recommend increased stock weights before market appreciation's and decreased weights before market declines. Examination of the performance of 326 newsletter asset-allocation strategies for the 1983-95 period shows that as a group, newsletters do not appear to possess any special information about the future direction of the market.

A second study by Roger Blake and Meir Statman looked at the reasons why letter writers changed their market opinion at various times. They found that movements in the market affect writer opinions and *not the other way around*. In other word, the letter writers as a group were following the market instead of leading it. The study also found excess market volatility caused rapid changes in opinion, while low volatility caused a slow but gradual change.[25] Newsletter writers are basically trend followers who prefer to drive forward by looking in the rear-view mirror. That causes many accidents.

---

24. John R. Graham and Campbell R. Harvey, Grading the Performance of Market-Timing Newsletters, *Financial Analyst's Journal,* Nov/Dec 1997
25. Roger G. Clarke and Meir Statman, Bullish or Bearish?, *Financial Analyst's Journal*, May/June 1998

Professional Money Managers and Market Timing

I am certainly not going to predict what general business or the stock market are going to do in the next year or two, since I don't have the faintest idea.
—Warren Buffett, Letter to Partners, 1963

Are professional fund managers able to predict the market better than Wall Street analysts? Do they possess skill or information the public does not have? There are dozens of academic studies on this subject. Measuring a fund manager's ability to time the market can be conducted in one of two ways. The researcher can measure the level of cash held by a mutual fund at various turning points in the market, or he can measure the level of risk the manager was taking at those times.

Mutual Fund Cash Levels

The amount of cash held in a mutual fund can yield important information about a manager's market timing ability. When a manager believes the market is overvalued, he typically sells stocks and raises cash. This cushions the portfolio against loss and prepares the fund for an increase in shareholder redemption. If the manager believes the market is headed higher, he buys stocks and reduces his company's cash position. This enables the firm to capture the higher return of stocks.

The Investment Company Institute (ICI) tracks the cash position of mutual funds and has data going back to early 1980s. Prior to the market crash of 1987, the average stock fund held steady at about 9.0% cash. There was no attempt to raise cash prior to the sell-off. *After* the crash, managers increased their cash position to 11% because they were anticipating further declines. The market quickly stabilized and produced significant gains in 1988 and 1989, and managers reduced their cash position back to the 9.0% level. Managers were late on both sides of the crash. They were late getting out of the market in 1987 and late getting back in during the recovery.

Let's look at a different period of time. In late 1990, during the buildup to Desert Storm, the stock market sold off, and managers increased cash to 11%. When the war began in mid-January 1991, the stock market surged and caught the managers with a large cash position. Over the decade managers gradually reduced the cash in their portfolios. By 1999, after the greatest bull market in history, cash positions were at a historic low of 4.0%.

The data clearly show that mutual fund managers change cash positions *after* the market changes direction, not before. They react to market movements; they do not anticipate them. The idea that an active manager will "get you out" of a market before it falls is simply marketing hype. There is no evidence to support that claim.

Mutual Fund Risk Levels

Another method of determining if managers can correctly predict market direction is to look at the risk of the securities in the portfolios. If a manager expects the stock market to move higher, she should increase the number of risky stocks in the portfolio to capture a return higher than the general market (technology stocks). If she believes the market is heading lower, risky stocks should be sold in favor of conservative stocks (utility stocks).

A review of mutual fund risk studies can be found in *Investment Analysis and Portfolio Management,* a textbook written by Frank K. Rielly, University of Notre Dame.[26] Rielly reviewed a number of risk studies con-

26. Frank K. Rielly, *Investment Analysis and Portfolio Management,* Dryden Press, Third Edition, pg. 853-5

ducted over a number of years. He finds no convincing evidence that professional managers were able to capture higher returns by changing the risk of their portfolios prior to a market turn. Nor did any single manager exhibit consistent skill in this regard. Not surprisingly, Rielly concluded that portfolio managers have no market timing ability.

Market Timing and Individual Investors

So far we have learned that professionals have not been successful timing the markets, but how have individual investors fared? The general public seems to follow market timing on two levels. For the short run, the most recent trend and popular opinion influence decisions to get into or out of the market. For the long term, decisions are imbedded in political and economic events that effect the morale of the entire nation.

Short-term Market Timing

Short-term timing is emotional and reactionary. Typically, a person makes a change in asset allocation as a result of a sharp turn in the direction of the markets, which makes nervous. During volatile markets, people listen closely to "expert" advice they hear in the bathroom at work, or they may follow the recommendations of popular market gurus on TV. Whatever the trigger, short-term timing decisions are emotional; however, they are typically not permanent.

In a bull market investors are always skeptical that the market will continue higher. It is said that the stock market climbs a "wall of worry." On the other hand, during times of sharp market declines, many investors are sure the market will continue to go down, and they want to react. In times of fear, investors herd together and imagine the worst outcome. In his epic work, *The Crowd,* Gustave Le Bon explains why following the advice of others during a time of market volatility is not the wisest action:

> The very fact that crowds possess in common ordinary qualities explains why they can never accomplish acts demanding a high degree of intelligence...The truth is, they can only bring to bear in common on the work at hand those mediocre qualities which is the birthright of every average individual. In crowds it is stupidity and not mother-wit that is accumulated.[27]

Watching the flow of public money into and out of mutual funds is a good way to study short-term timing. Studies of mutual fund cash flows during volatile market conditions reflect popular opinion of the markets. In 1987, after the stock market crash, redemption of stock in mutual funds increased significantly, and exchanges into bond funds went up dramatically.[28] A similar reaction occurred in 1990.

Stephen Nesbitt of Wilshire Associates studied mutual fund cash flows to measure the effect of market timing on returns.[29] His goal was to measure the cost of market timing to investors by measuring the movement of money between broad categories of mutual funds, i.e. moving from stock funds to bond funds. Nesbitt's research covered a period of ten years, from 1984 through mid 1994. He found the average investor lost about 1.0% each per year due to sector switching, not

---

27. Gustave Le Baron, *The Crowd: A Study of the Popular Mind,* Cherokee Publishing Co., Marietta, GA, pg. 9
28. ICI data on equity and fixed income mutual fund cash flow. 1984 -1998
29. Stephen L. Nesbitt, "Buy High, Sell Low: Timing Errors in Mutual Fund Allocations," *Journal of Portfolio Management,* Fall 1995, pg. 57-60

including commission costs. As investors try to time the markets, either intentionally or unintentionally, they lose money. It is best to choose your level of risk and stay invested over the long term. Chapter 14 covers this concept in detail.

Long-term Market Timing

Over a lifetime stocks outperform bonds, and bonds outperform money market funds. Therefore, most people should invest a large portion of their lifetime savings in the stock market. Right? Not quite. While this advice works well in a bull market, the public has a totally different opinion about the future when major political and economic disruptions cause fear and uncertainty. Those events cause structural changes in our lives, which are typically reflected by a prolonged bear market for stocks.

Two important periods of time should be studied by every stock investor. These are the period following the crash of 1929, and the period following the market meltdown of 1973-74. These two periods offer clues as to how people shift their investment behavior following a period of political turmoil and deep bear markets. The following data is complied from Federal Reserve records, the Investment Company Institute, the New York Stock Exchange, and other sources. Analysis of this information clearly reveals one trend: the public will abandon the stock market when a major negative event happens. I have no idea what that event will be or when it will occur.

Major Investor Shifts from 1900 to 1999

In 1896 *The Wall Street Journal* began publishing the Dow Jones Index on a daily basis. It was a composite of the twelve best-known stocks at the time. Though the market was volatile, and stock manipulation was common, the number of stock market investors was steadily increasing. The stock market boomed in the 1920s, fueled by speculation and borrowed money. Over 10% of the working population joined in the fun and bought common stocks.[30]

The crash of 1929 came slowly at first. Then, following a Federal Reserve tightening and Congressional tax increase, the stock market collapsed. The market fell 82% from its high, and many people could not pay their margin loans. As a result, banks collapsed, sending the economy into a tailspin and throwing the country into period of despair. The public left the stock market in droves.

The experience of the 1929 crash stayed on the minds of Americans until the end of the Korean War. By that time public ownership of stocks was at a low of 4.0%. The turnaround came in the early 1950s as a new generation of investors emerged. As the stock market moved higher, more investors became involved. During this period, brokerage firms were busy expanding their reach to every city and town. Investment salesmen went door to door selling stocks and a new product called "mutual funds."

By 1972, stocks as a percent of household financial assets hit 38%. Over 16% of the adult population owned stocks, more than any other time in history. Unfortunately, as a result of the Vietnam War, the dollar began to suffer, and growing political pressure caused President Nixon to take the country off the gold standard in 1973. This major shift in policy caused the dollar to collapse and inflation to surge. Between 1973 and 1974, the S&P 500 fell 42%. The rapid decline drove many inves-

---

30. Charles R. Geisst, *Wall Street: A History,* Oxford University Press, New York, 1997

tors out of the stock market, and they stayed out until the early 1990s.

Although stocks had compounded a 15.5% annual return from 1982 to 1992, few new investors entered the market. Finally, in the early 1990s, a third generation of investors came aboard. Baby boomers became a major force driving Wall Street. Low inflation and the popularity of mutual funds fueled the growth. Today there are more stock investors as a percent of the adult population than ever before. Stocks have grown to over 40% of household financial assets, a new record.

The following chart puts a lot of this information in graphic form. It compares the rolling five-year return of the S&P 500 from 1950 through mid 1998 with the percent of household financial assets in stocks and stock mutual funds. For the entire period, the average household held 24% of their financial assets in stocks. However, the mix was constantly changing. Stocks ranged from 11% in 1982 to 40% in 1998.

Using this data, we can estimate the cost of long-term market timing decisions on a generation of investors. Had the public maintained a constant 24% in stocks during the entire 1950-98 period, the annualized return on the stock portion of their portfolio would have been 13.2% (using the S&P 500 as a benchmark). Due to the effects of market timing decisions over a generation, the model produced a return of only 12.2%. Long-term shifts in investor beliefs brought about by political and economic upheaval lowered the investor returns by 1.0% annually.

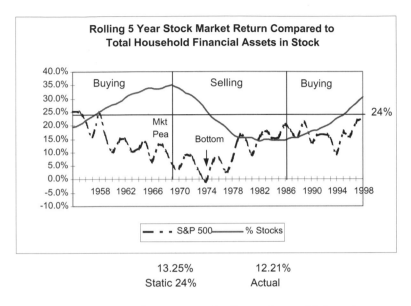

Rolling 5 Year Stock Market Return Compared to Total Household Financial Assets in Stock

13.25%	12.21%
Static 24%	Actual

How long the current bull market will last is anyone's guess. Some people believe baby boomers will maintain a high exposure to stocks even during a prolonged economic crisis. I do not believe that. When the tide turns, there is doubt how investors will react. The general public did not hold onto stocks after the crash in 1929, nor did they hold after the bear market of 1973-74, and they will certainly sell again in the future. This will have an adverse effect on investor performance in the long run.

Conclusion

This rather long chapter explained the two ways market timing contributes to the performance gap between market returns and investor returns. Short-term timing decisions lower results by about 1.0% per year (not including trading costs or the tax consequences) and long-term decisions take away more returns. The combined cost of all market timing decisions is estimated at 1.5% to 2.0% per year *over an investor's lifetime*. It is very difficult to maintain a set allocation to stocks during adverse conditions, but it certainly pays to do so.

Chapter 6

Chasing the Hot Dot

Fortune turns round like a millwheel, and he who was yesterday at the top, lies today at the bottom.
—Miguel De Cervantes

Investing in the financial markets requires you to make a number of decisions. First, you must decide *which* market to invest in, such as the stock market, and then decide how much to put in it. Next, you must decide how you will invest in that market. Should you buy individual stocks or a stock mutual fund? Last, you must decide which stocks or mutual funds to purchase. The selection of individual investments is the subject of this chapter. The largest portion of the performance gap can be traced to investor behavior during the security selection process.

Chasing the hot dot is a phrase used to describe the behavior of most people when choosing investments. This is a method of selection based solely on a review of past performance. Though few people, especially financial advisers, will admit to relying solely on past performance when choosing investments, everyone relies on past performance to some extent. Chasing the hot dot can be a costly mistake. Studies conclude that investors who base their decisions firmly on recent performance typically experience low returns.

Despite this fact, each year billions of dollars flow into mutual funds with the best short-term performance. While an investment in these funds seems astute at the time, the out-performance does not persist. Styles go in and out of favor, and a strategy of buying the top performers eventually leads to increased volatility and below average results. The negative results of chasing the hot dot may not be evident in the short-term, especially if the style stays in favor for a year or so, but over a lifetime of investing, moving from one investment to another based mainly on past performance can significantly increase the performance gap.

An Example of Chasing the Hot Dot

PBHG Growth Fund was a very popular mutual fund in the mid-1990s. For three years ending in 1995, PBHG Growth was up over 100%, placing it on top of the mutual fund rankings. Several leading newspapers and magazines interviewed Gary Pilgrim and crowned him a bona fide stock-picking guru. Investment advisors and newsletter writers across the country where quick to add his fund to their recommended list. The attention helped triple the assets in his fund over the next year.

PBHG Growth Fund Comparison

Calendar Year	Assets in Millions at the Beginning of the Year	Performance Relative to the S&P 500
1993	3	36.7%
1994	184	3.4%
1995	746	12.8%
1996	2,028	(13.1%)
1997	5,931	(36.7%)
1998	5,464	(28.0%)

Source: Morningstar, Inc.

From its inception in 1985 through year end 1992, PBHG Growth Fund had mediocre performance, and few people had ever heard of Gary Pilgrim. In 1993 there were only three million dollars in his fund. Fortunes changed overnight, and during the next three years Pilgrim had one of the hottest hands in the business. As a result, money gushed in. By the end of 1995, PBHG Growth Fund had accumulated over two billion dollars in assets, most of it from new investors. Then the tide began to turn. The fund underperformed the market by 13% in 1996.

Despite the lackluster performance, the three-year results still placed PBHG Growth on top of the performance rankings. Money continued to flow in at an unprecedented pace. By January 1997, PBHG Growth had close to six billion dollars in assets. Then the storm really struck. During the first quarter of 1997, the fund dropped nearly 20% in value, losing shareholders nearly 1.2 billion dollars. For the entire year the fund registered a return almost 37% below the S&P 500. Poor performance continued into 1998. The fund under-achieved the market by another 28%.

For ten years ending 1998, PBHG had returns in line with the S&P 500. Unfortunately, the best years occurred when there was little money in the fund. As a general rule, the greatest amount of money flows into the hottest sectors and the hottest funds at precisely the wrong time. Many investors in PBHG *lost* money from 1996-98 and many others missed three fabulous years in the stock market. This example clearly shows how chasing the hot dot causes a wide performance gap. It is common to find similar circumstances in other funds and fund categories.

PBHG Was Not Alone

In 1994, Morningstar conducted a cash flow study of all US growth funds. They included 219 funds in the study and covered a five-year period between 1989 and 1994. The purpose was to compare the return of the growth fund category with the actual profits made by investors in the funds. Cash flows into and out of each individual fund were calculated in a manner similar to the DAL-BAR study you read about in Chapter 3.

The average growth fund earned an annual return of 12.5% during the period. However, Morningstar calculated that the average investor in those funds lost 2.2% during the same time period. The reported 12.5% return of the category had little bearing on investor success. Investor behavior *within* the category had the greatest impact on returns. Investors shifted money in and out of funds at the wrong time, and their profits never materialized. Chasing the hot dot caused investors to lose while the entire market gained.

Tracking the Performance of Past Winners

Selecting an investment based on superior performance is the same as selecting a line to stand in at the supermarket. The moment you jump in one line, it stops moving.

—Rick Ferri

In 1988 CDA Technologies conducted a ten-year study of 363 mutual funds to see if past performance could be used to choose winning investment strategies. They ranked mutual funds by their five-year returns from 1977 to 1981 and compared them to the next five years. Of the top twenty funds in the first five-year period, not one of those funds was in the top twenty during the second five-year period and only two made it into the top

100. As a group, the top twenty funds from the first period ranked 222 during the second period, well below average. Based on CDA data, purchasing a mutual fund based on prior five-year performance leads to poor results.

In 1994 Morningstar conducted a similar study. Consistent with the CDA study, the top performing categories the first period were at the bottom category the next period.

Performance by Category

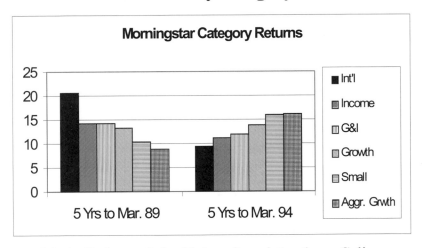

Mark Carhart of the University of Southern California, recently conducted a landmark study of the persistence of mutual fund returns. He found a small tendency for the very best funds to continue their performance for a short while after a superior year, but any excess return generated by holding the top funds did not last more than one year. By the third year of the five-year period selected for the study, the top funds fell into the below-average category. In addition, there was more risk in buying the top funds. When the top funds fall, they do so very quickly, and many go straight to the bottom of the rankings. Carhart also concluded that fund expenses had a large impact on return, and the worst funds within a category tended to be those with the highest fees.[31]

In 1996 Morningstar conducted an interesting study comparing "popular" fund categories with "unpopular" funds. A popular fund category style was characterized as taking in the most money over the preceding twelve-month period. Unpopular funds had the worst money flow. In the year that followed, over 80% of the unpopular funds performed better than the popular ones.[32] As a general rule, mutual fund styles *regress to the mean*. This means that over time, the performances of all investment styles tend to merge.[33] If investors flock to styles that have recently surged, they have already missed most of the upside of the variation and are more likely to capture the regression backwards.

Investors Continue to Chase the Hot Dot

Although evidence against chasing the hot funds and hot styles is overwhelming, investors still prefer top performers to everything else. A survey conducted by Montgomery Asset Management in San Francisco found that 63% of investor's list superior performance as the number one reason for choosing a fund.[34] Researchers at Columbia University's Graduate School of Business found that investors choose past performance two-to-one over any other method of fund selec-

---

31. Mark M. Carhart, "On the Persistence of Mutual Fund Performance," *Journal of Finance*, Mar. 1997, Vol. LII, No. 1, pg. 57-82.
32. Susan Paluch and Jeff Kelly, Going Against the Crowd, Morningstar Mutual Funds, Jan. 1996, Vol. 4, Number 5.
33. John Bogle, *Bogle on Mutual Funds,* Dell Publishing, NY, 1994, pg. 92
34. As reported in *Dow Jones Asset Management*, May/June 1997

tion. As a result, over 90% of all new investment money flows into mutual funds with the top ratings by Morningstar, while those with the lowest rating lose assets.[35]

Using Star Ratings and other Devices to Pick Mutual Funds

As the sheer number of mutual funds grows, so does the business of mutual fund ratings. The slicing and dicing of mutual fund returns has become a huge, competitive industry. Of the companies in the game, the largest and most popular are Morningstar Mutual Funds in Chicago, Lipper Analytical Services in Summit, NJ, and Value Line Mutual Funds.

Most private rating agencies use star ratings and other designations to rank mutual funds. Morningstar and Lipper are quick to point out that their rankings have no predictive value, and that this was not the intent of the rating system. Morningstar editor Amy C. Arnott wrote about misuse of their rating system:

> Over the years, Morningstar's star system has been frequently—and sometimes willfully— misunderstood. Many commentators insist on treating the star rating as a predictive measure or a short-term trading signal. The rating, which is clearly labeled as a historical profile, does neither.[36]

Right or wrong, the investment industry sells their products based on a favorable Morningstar rating. You see the ads in every commercial investment publication.

---

35. Karen Damato, "Morningstar Edges Toward One-Year Ratings," *The Wall Street Journal,* April 5, 1996, pg. C1.
36. Amy C. Arnott, Editor, Beyond the Stars: The New Category Rating, Morningstar Mutual Funds, Summary Section, Dec. 6, 1996, vol. 29, issue 2.

Open any Money magazine and you will find several examples of how Morningstar and Lipper rankings are misused by investment companies. In addition, brokers and other financial advisors use mutual fund rankings to imply that their ideas have merit. Generally, a highly rated fund helps make the sale easier. The attitude is "if the public believes that star ratings or past performance predicts the future, then let them believe it."

Morningstar is first to admit that their rankings should not be used to predict performance; nevertheless, competitor Lipper Analytical couldn't resist discrediting their rating system. In 1994, Lipper examined Morningstar's five-star funds from 1990 to 1993 and found that their top ratings did not translate to top performance. Lipper found a majority of 5-star funds performed below average after they received their rating.[37]

The *Hulbert Financial Digest* newsletter also tracked Morningstar's five-star funds. The study found that the funds lagged the market by a sizable margin. The average five-star funds rose 28.9% during the 32-month period while the Wilshire 5000 stock index rose 59.5% and the Lehman Brothers Treasury bond composite gained 36.9%. Mark Hulbert has also found the average five-star fund retained its rating for only five months.[38] Morningstar's Arnott was correct: the star ratings have no predictive value.

Owning Several Funds May Not Solve the Problem

It is a common belief that holding several mutual funds in a portfolio lowers overall risk. A diversification strat-

---

37. Selling the Future, Concerns About Misuse of Mutual Fund Ratings, Lipper Analytical Services, Inc., Summit, NJ, May 16, 1994
38. Mark Hulbert, *Forbes*, December 6, 1993, pg. 275

egy works to reduce risk only when the mutual funds are of sufficiently different styles. Many investors falsely assume that their portfolio is well diversified simply because they hold several funds. The 401(k) plans of the Big Three auto makers offer dozens of mutual funds, many with similar styles. After the growth stock boom in the late 1990s it was common to find participants "diversifying" among four or five *large-cap growth stock* funds, ignoring all other categories. Buying different funds of the same style is not diversification.

There is a logical reason why many investors do not diversify their mutual fund holdings. Few people have any knowledge of investment styles. In a recent survey Columbia University researchers asked investors to describe what category of funds they owned. Three out of four (75%) of investors did not know if they were in a fixed income funds or stock funds, and 72% did not know if they were in a US stock fund or an international fund.[39] Most people simply invest in the funds that have performed the best over the last few years, regardless of style or category.

In 1993, emerging country funds were hot. Some funds were up more than 80% for the year. As a result, in early 1994 more than half of all new stock mutual fund money flowed into emerging country funds. As you might expect, over next four years the emerging country funds collapsed, and many investors sustained large losses.

---

39. Noel Capon, Gavan J. Fitzsimmons, and Russell Alan Price, An Individual Analysis of the Mutual Fund Investment Decision, Columbia University Graduate School of Business working paper.

Individual Stock Investors Also Chase Returns

Nothing captures interest faster or keeps it at a higher level than the mouth-watering thought of a profit. If the potential is large, your prospects interest focuses sharply on your next comments.[40]

—Lerory Gross

Thus far we have addressed only mutual funds investors, but many people still take the old-fashioned route: they build individual stock portfolios. What common habits do these investors exhibit? As a group, they buy and sell roughly the same stocks during the same time, with little influencing their decisions except short-term price momentum, media hype, and popular opinion.[41] Several independent studies confirm these investing habits.[42]

Why do individual investors go for risky stocks and generally ignore Blue Chip companies? "Those are too big, too boring, and everyone already knows the story," says G.M. Loeb in his 1935 classic book, *The Battle for Investment Survival.* Loeb explains:

> It is characteristic for the novice investor to want to run before he has learned to crawl, or walk. Tell a beginner to buy one of the best-known listed stocks as his first equity venture

---

40. Le Roy Gross, *Art of Selling Intangibles: How to Make Your Million$ Investing Other People's Money,* New York Institute of Finance, NY, 1988, pg. 71, Gross's book was written for stockbrokers. His techniques are widely used throughout the brokerage industry.

41. Terrance Odean, University of California at Berkeley, as reported in *Registered Representative* magazine, July 1997, pg. 38

42. Robert J. Shiller, *Market Volatility,* First MIT Press, 1997, pg. 376

and you get a look of scorn for such kindergarten ideas...Talk about the pitfalls in new, unseasoned, small, or relatively obscure stocks and get brushed off for your pains. The blue-ribbon roster of America's most successful corporations might be good enough for our best institutions, but somehow fail to interest the tyro...He feels incorrectly that he must buy something "new," something "special," or something "exclusive" with him.[43]

Terrance Odean of the University of California concluded that most investors sell winning stocks before large gains develop. He analyzed thousands of individual accounts at a discount brokerage and found investors twice as likely to sell winners over losers. This reduced returns by a considerable amount each year.[44] Jeremy Siegal of the Wharton School came to a similar conclusion. He estimates individual stock investors perform about 5.0% less than the market as a whole.[45] Siegal assumed that investor's stayed 100% in stocks and did not time the market. From evaluating hundreds of investor-managed stock accounts over the years, I have found that investors perform at least 5.0% below the market.

Summary of this Chapter and Part I

The erosion of returns in a portfolio from chasing the hot dot is a gradual process. It takes several years before the effects are evident. Since most people hold a fund

---

43. G.M. Loeb, *The Battle for Investment Survival,* Simon and Schuster, NY, 1935, pg 281
44. Odean.
45. Jeremy J. Siegal, *Stocks for the Long Run,* Irwin Press, 1994, pg 292.

for three to five years, they tend to forget what drew them to the fund to begin with. However, when they do decide to move to other investment, it is almost always news of recent superior performance that draws them in. Peter Lynch had this to say about chasing the hot dot in his second book, *Beating the Street*:[46]

> How do you chose a value fund, growth fund, or capital appreciation fund that will outdo its rivals? Most people look at past performance. They study the Lipper guide published in *Barron's* or any one of a number of similar sources that track fund performance. They look at the record for 1 year, 3 years, 5 years, and beyond. This is another national pastime, reviewing the past performance of funds. Thousands of hours are devoted to it. Books and articles are written about it. Yet with few exceptions, this turns out to be a waste of time.

It is not the action of the stock or bond market that leads to the large performance gap; it is the cost of investing in those markets and the behavior of investors that cause the gap. Fees, commissions, market timing, and investment selection errors significantly reduce returns over the long term.

Straight talk about the antics of Wall Street will help set your portfolio straight. Part II of this book explains why the financial services industry supports ill-fated investment strategies, and why market "experts" are usually more of a hindrance than a help.

---

46. Peter Lynch, *Beating the Street*, Simon and Schuster, NY, 1993, pgs 67,68

PART II

Investment Experts and Other Barriers to Success

Chapter 7

Mass Market Investment Advice: A Recipe for Mediocrity

Don't kid yourself about selling. People are motivated by two things; fear and greed. They are afraid to lose what they have and they are greedy to get more.[47]

—Bert Cornfield

Ask any investment advisor why you should be in the stock market and you will hear this response: "Because over the long term stocks produce higher returns than bonds or money market funds." They will likely point to historic charts and graphs to prove their point.

Advisors are correct about the return of stocks. Over time stocks do produce higher returns than bonds or money funds. But when they talk about the investment potential of stocks, most advisors are referring to the *stock market.* Since this is the case, it would be logical for almost everyone to invest in stock *index funds,* since index funds are drawn from all stocks offered within the market and therefore enjoy a return that matches the performance of the stock market. Unfortu-

47. Bent Cantor, *The Bernie Cornfield Story,* Lyle Stuart, NY, 1970, pg. 16-17

nately, this is not what happens. A major breakdown occurs in the investing process as soon as a person asks the advisor, "How should I invest in the stock market?" Part II of this book explains what many investment advisors recommend—and the problems that exist in their recommendations.

A Conflict of Interest

In Part I of this book we explained three broad reasons why individual investors experience significantly lower returns that the markets they invest in. High expenses, poor market timing decisions, and chasing the hot dot have resulted in a wide performance gap. Part II of this report looks at how the investment industry and mass media *encourage* investors to behave in a manner that causes that performance gap. We will look at the sellers of investment advice and how their personal goals conflict with the goals of investors.

Wall Street is an exciting place. It represents free markets, capitalism, and opportunity for everyone. But it is also wrought with false promises and questionable sales practices. Whether you are working with a stockbroker or reading an investment magazine, you are faced with the daunting task of separating fact from fiction in an industry whose primary goal is to make money *from* you, not *for* you.

Where the Public Gets Investment Advice

Individual investors generally get their advice from three places: the popular press (including the Internet), friends and relatives, and paid advisors. In 1998, Kansas City-based American Century conducted telephone surveys of several hundred individual investors, and asked them to list their sources of investment advice.[48] The source mentioned most often was the financial press, including magazines, newspapers, TV, and the Internet. Other top sources of advice were friends and family, and paid advisors. The findings of this study are summarized in the following chart.

Where Investors Obtain Advice

Source of Advice	% Mentioned
Financial media	44%
Friends and family	39%
Accountants and tax advisor	32%
Independent financial planners	29%
Stockbrokers	28%
Bankers	25%

In 1997 the NASDAQ Stock Exchange conducted a similar survey of individual investors who considered themselves "well informed." NASDAQ asked the group where they got their investment information. About 38% said they read *The Wall Street Journal* daily and 23% read *Money* magazine each month. Close to 38% reported watching TV shows like Wall Street Week or listening to radio talk shows. Only 20% said they looked to their local newspaper for advice, down from 58% in 1985.

As far as the human touch goes, informed investors rely heavily on professional advice, with brokers and other financial consultants leading the pack.

Professional Advisors of "Well Informed" Investors

Personal Advisor	% Mentioned
Stockbrokers (including financial planners)	52%
Friends and relatives	51%
Accountants	43%
Bankers	38%

As you can garner from the answers above, most people use two or three sources of investment information when managing their portfolios. Some of the advice comes from print, some from radio, TV and the Internet, some from friends and relatives, and some from advisors. Are these sources of information unbiased? Do they give you all the facts? Not by a long shot. Most advice is either vague or incomplete. It takes a clear mind to sort out even one or two relevant facts from the noise.

It is interesting to note what's missing from the surveys. No one mentioned investment courses offered through local colleges and universities. Many places of higher education run informative, non-sales oriented classes on financial planning and investment management. The classroom is a great place to obtain less biased investment information.

Perhaps the public believes the advice they are getting outside of academia comes from knowledgeable and properly educated people. That would be a dangerous assumption, and potentially a costly one. We will learn in later chapters that many people in the investment advice industry are not well trained and are certainly not experts.

A Recipe for Mediocrity

For a long time I have not said what I believe, nor do I believe what I say, and if indeed I do happen to tell the truth, I hide it among so many lies that it is hard to find.
—Machiavelli in a letter to Fancesco Guicciardini, May 17, 1521

Most investment advice sold *en masse* to the public is a recipe for mediocrity. The advice tends to revolve around the concept of "beating the market." While it is possible that mass market advice may lead to superior returns in the short run, it is destined to fail in the long term. It is not conceivable that the majority of investors beat the market, especially after fees and expense. Yet "beat the market" advice is in demand, and the burgeoning investment industry finds the demand for this advice to be very profitable.

However, by the time an investment idea makes its way to the general public, the idea is old. There may be some momentum in the markets that carry the idea forward for a while, but in the long run the public is always late to the game. The markets adjust so fast that individual investors have little chance to capitalize on new information. Stockbrokers and investment advisors may be one small step ahead of the public, but that makes little difference. Most advisors are not skilled enough to make superior investment decisions.

Since almost everyone has access to the same market information at about the same time, only *opinions* and *interpretations* differ. These opinions appear all around you in the form of newspaper articles, analysts' comments, advice from CNN, and your broker. Some opinions sound more credible than others, and some people may be able to accurately interpret the news and profit from it, but overall the markets adjust too quickly for the any individual investor to consistently capitalize on new ideas.

Does anyone get better information? Although it is not supposed to happen, institutional investors with large holdings in a stock may have access to information before it becomes public knowledge. Al Dunlap, former CEO of Scott Paper and Sunbeam, clearly explains this in his book, *Mean Business*. Dunlap wrote, "A small investor doesn't have access to the information and resources Soros does."[49] He was referring to private meetings between Scott Paper and an investment group representing hedge fund manager George Soros. The hedge fund made a large profit when Dunlap sold Scott Paper to Kimberly Clark. However, institutional investors do not always profit from extra information. Many institutions lost a bundle when Dunlap could not find a buyer for Sunbeam and the company collapsed.

A Preview of the Chapters in Part II

Part II of this book refutes the marketing claims of the sellers of investment products and advice. There are no superior methods of investing that "beat the street" consistently. Advisors and other investment "experts" that sell such market strategies have an ulterior motive— making money for themselves. I have found no evidence that beat-the-market advice works, only that following it leads to mediocre results.

Preview of Chapter 8— The Myth of Investment Experts

The public has a little knowledge of the way Wall Street works. Large brokerage firms have hundreds of analysts covering thousands of investments plus dozens of economists following the economic beat. This impressive

---

49. Albert J. Dunlap, *Mean Business*, Fireside, NY, 1997, pg. 264

network of brainpower may give investors the impression that their stockbroker or advisor is very knowledgeable and offers superior advice. This impression is typically far from reality.

Most advisors who consult directly with individual investors are not highly trained nor are they knowledgeable in an academic sense. A large majority of stockbrokers, financial planners, insurance people, and independent advisors are strictly salespeople whose training is limited to firms they sell for. Chapter 8 looks at the people we turn to for investment advice and exposes a major shortfall that exists in the education and training of most "investment professionals."

Preview of Chapter 9–
The Persuasive Power of the Press

Selling investment advice via the printing press is a multi-million dollar business. There are now dozens of newsstand publications that offer investment advice for $2.50 or less. Unfortunately, most of the information in these publications is based on market hype and strategies encouraging readers to engage in *chasing the hot dot*, described in Chapter 6.

Some journalists who work for large, established publishers are well educated in financial subjects, while many others lack elementary knowledge about the economics and the markets. Reporters frequently quote investment "experts" in their stories. Ironically, many publications only interview "experts" who advertise in their publication, regardless of their skill or knowledge.

Investment books are a different animal. The best books are based on years of academic research and practical experience. Legendary investor Peter Lynch wrote two books about beating Wall Street at its own game. While these books were entertaining, I doubt any reader "beat the street" as a result. Even Peter Lynch himself admits that it is a very difficult undertaking and that the idea of owning the entire market through a low-cost *index fund* has a lot of appeal. Unfortunately, many books are of the get-rich-quick variety. Authors whose main intention is to make money for themselves, not their readers, write these books.

A Preview of Chapter 10—
Mutual Fund Follies

In 1946 Ed Johnson, then president of Fidelity Investments, explained to the SEC that beating the market is not the goal of his company. He told the SEC, "The management has no illusions it can beat the market and does not try...rotation of investments often occurs."[50]

Fidelity's business plan was to create dozens of funds, pushing the good ones and closing the bad ones. Ned Johnson, Ed's son and subsequent president of Fidelity, would begin a new fund even if he would not put one nickel of his own money into it.[51] The multiple fund strategy has worked for Fidelity Investments, the nation's largest fund company. As of 1998, Fidelity offered over 100 funds of which 57 are stock funds.

Mutual fund companies have become the leading investment choice for individual investors. Since beating the market is difficult, successful fund companies have learned that the key to the business is based on opening new funds in hot sectors, and having a strong marketing plan. By offering dozens of funds, a firm hopes one or two will be a winner, so they can exploit those funds and gather assets.

---

50. Daina B. Henriques, *Fidelities World*, Scribner, NY, 1991, pg. 105
51. Ibid, pg. 234, interview with Mark Shenkman, a former money manager at Fidelity.

Summary

Do not confuse the goals of the investment industry with your own goals. While there are many fine people working in the field, the real goal of the industry is to make money *from* you, not *for* you. As a result, most mass-market investment advice encourages behavior that *widens* the performance gap. As long as investors continue to seek superior returns, they will continue to pay commissions, buy subscriptions to investment magazines and newspapers, seek the advice of a paid advisor, and purchase an assortment of other products and services provided by the investment industry. This is a recipe for mediocrity.

Chapter 8

The Myth of Investment Experts

None of our men are "experts." We have unfortunately found it necessary to get rid of a man as soon as he thinks himself an expert because no one ever considers himself expert if he knows his job.

—Henry Ford

Investment experts can be found everywhere, especially during a bull market. Are you looking for expert advice? The next time you are at a social gathering just mention to a few people that you are interested in the stock market but know little about it. More experts than you ever imagined will soon surround you.

The number of paid investment advisors has proliferated to nauseating proportions. During the 1990s more people entered the investment advice business than at any previous time in history. Since 1990 the number of registered stockbrokers has grown to hundreds of thousands. The number of advisors explodes when you add financial planners, independent advisors, and insurance agents. If that isn't enough, thousands of accountants, lawyers, and bankers now offer investment advice in addition to their core services.

With so many people offering their investment expertise you do not have to search for an advisor; one will find you. However, if you are looking for a truly competent advisor, it may take a lot of time and effort.

The level of knowledge and experience varies greatly in the industry. Unfortunately, the average advisor has a level of expertise that is disgustingly low. Few have any educational background beyond the simple exams required to get into the business. To put the industry in perspective, more training is required for a 16-year-old to get a driver's license than for a person to become a registered financial advisor.

Types of Investment Advisors

There are three broad categories of advisors that work with individual investors. They are classified as traditional stockbrokers, financial planners (FP), and registered investment advisors (RIA). Insurance salespeople and banks fall under the realm of stockbrokers because they generally work on commission. Accountants and attorneys fall normally fall under the RIA category because they collect management fees. As you read the different descriptions below you will notice there is a blurry line between brokers, financial planners, and independent advisors. In many ways the blur is by design. Advisors want to be whatever their clients want them to be, and titles change frequently. Nevertheless, in one way or another all advisors are paid base on the products and services they sell, not the quality of advice they provide.

Stockbrokers

There are over 60,000 active stockbrokers registered today working for national and regional firms. There are also thousands of brokers claiming to be independent, but that is a misnomer. All registered brokers must place their license with a brokerage firm that is a member of the New York Stock Exchange (NYSE). The average stockbroker at a national firm made about $150,000 in

1998, and the top five percent made over one million. The large financial rewards lure many into the field, but the competition is intense and the survival rate is low. Only sixty percent of stockbrokers survive the first three years in business and far less are around after five.[52]

Since turnover is so high, there is always a need for new brokers, and there are so few requirements to enter the field. First, you need to be sponsored by an active broker-dealer. Some large brokerage firms require full employment while many small firms will sponsor you as an independent. Next, you need to take the Series 7 Registered Representative exam offered through the National Association of Securities Dealers (NASD). The application to qualify for the exam asks about criminal records, lawsuits, liens, and other problems you may have had. It *does not* ask about your experience or education background in the investment field. After a few weeks of study and possibly a crash course on the subject, you pass the Series 7 exam. Now you are fully qualified to sell investment products and services to the public. You are an *investment professional.*

Very few people in the industry call themselves a stockbroker anymore. Ten years ago brokers sold mostly investment products; now they sell everything from checking accounts to home mortgages. Because of their expanded role, brokers created many new titles. These names include Financial Consultant, Financial Advisor, Investment Counselor, Investment Partner, and even Personal CFO.

Regardless of the name change, most brokers are still paid the old-fashioned way, by commissions and fees. Few advisors are paid strictly by salary. As a result, *it is impossible for brokers to offer objective advice since their personal income is tied so closely to the*

---

52. Mark Sutton, director of Pain Webber's private client group, *On Wall Street*, January 1998, pg. 20.

products they sell. I was a broker for ten years and this is an absolute fact. The conflict of interest that exists between offering objective investment advice and getting paid is overpowering.

Financial Planners

The title Financial Planner (FP) has also become a misnomer. Years ago financial planners only wrote detailed financial plans for clients at an hourly rate fee or flat fee. They did not sell investment products or directly manage their client's money. Nowadays, for better or worse, FP means much more. Like stockbrokers, most FPs are interested in selling investment products rather than offer financial planning advice. Although most FPs still offer financial plans, they only do it the extent that it leads to a product sale or an ongoing advisory relationship.

A commission-based planner goes through the securities exam process and sells investment products through a designated licensed broker-dealer. They are, in a sense, independent stockbrokers, but they prefer to call themselves financial planners for marketing reasons. Insurance agents also fall under this category because they are paid a commission to sell investment products.

The second type of FP is typically called a "fee-only" planner, although the "fee" is no longer for a writing a comprehensive financial plan. This type of planner is looking to be paid an ongoing annual fee for managing clients' assets. Fee-only planners typically use no-load mutual fund "wrap" programs to accomplish this objective (see Chapter 4). They meet with clients on a regular basis to discuss the performance of the funds and make necessary changes. Accountants and attorneys generally fall under the fee-only type of advisor, although in many instances they do not actually make the investment decisions themselves. They may refer clients to an outside advisor and split the fee.

If you are going to use a financial planner, I recommend searching for a "traditional" one. Go to someone who charges by the hour for financial advice and does not sell products. Traditional planners can help develop long-term investment strategies, review insurance needs, advise you on taxes, and help with estate planning. Just remember that there should be no conflict of interest between the planner and your plan. Look for someone with the Certified Financial Planner (CFP) designation and a four-year college degree in finance. This ensures that they have dedication to their practice.

Investment Advisors

If becoming a broker sounds easy, registering as an investment advisor is a snap. Almost anyone can claim to be a Registered Investment Advisor (RIA) and collect fees for investment management services. There are only a handful of rules and regulations that must be followed. Most states require applicants to pass a simple test. As of this writing the test does *not* cover investment concepts. It only covers procedures and laws surrounding the investment industry. Advisors with less than $25 million under management need register only with the states where they do business. Investment advisors who manage $25 million or more must register with the SEC, which means completing another application and sending in another fee. However, no further testing is required.

Registration does not mean Government approval or certification. Nor does it imply that the advisor is ethical or competent. Registration simply means the advisor has submitted the appropriate forms and has paid a filing fee. This is the same as registering an automobile with the Department of Transportation. Just because you registered a car does not mean that it runs or that you know how to drive it.

Since there are no barriers of entry to become and RIA, the field attracts all sorts of people. You will find former journalists, physicists, teachers, bankers, brokers, actors, and even Nobel Prize economists. In 1998, there were over 25,000 RIAs registered on with the SEC, and a great many smaller advisors registered with states across the country. Ironically, other than meeting additional registration requirements, very large investment advisors such as Fidelity are on equal footing with small firms such as Joe the Barber Investment Advisor.

Advisor Titles and Designations: The Good, the Bad, and the Worthless

Education and experience vary widely in the investment advice field. Many financial advisors may have minimal education and experience while others have extensive backgrounds and education. The only way to tell the difference is to ask for a resume and check credentials. Generally, at a minimum you are looking for at least an undergraduate degree in business or economics, plus a meaningful professional designation such as Certified Financial Planner (CFP) or Chartered Financial Analyst (CFA). Firm-designated titles such as Vice President or Senior Consultant are meaningless.

Designations

Many advisors have a lot of letters in back of their name. Typically, these take the form of acronyms such as CFA, CPF, CPA-MA, ChFC, CIMI, or something similar. Some titles are very prestigious. They require years of hard work, academic study, and job experience. Other titles are best described as Mickey Mouse. They are achieved by joining a marketing organization and paying an annual fee.

One recognized title is the Certified Financial Planner (CFP) designation. It signifies a well-rounded education in the area of personal finance. The program requires a candidate to complete five courses covering insurance, investments, estate planning, taxation, and many other issues. It usually takes a candidate eighteen months to complete the self-study program. The insurance industry has an equivalent designation called a ChFC, and the CPA community has a very distinguished title called CPA-MA.

A second prestigious designation pertaining mostly to Wall Street analysts and institutional money managers is the Chartered Financial Analyst (CFA) designation. The CFA requires several years of advanced academic study and practical experience. The CFA designation has the stature in the investment industry as a CPA in accounting, a JD in law, or an MD in the medical field.

After the designations noted above, the level of relevance drops off considerably, and the degree of work required to earn some of the designations is minimal at best. There are even mail-order titles that people can attain by taking a simple exam or joining a marketing organization. To their credit, most reputable Wall Street firms do not recognize purchased designations, and stockbrokers cannot place them on a business card. However, independent advisors are a different story. Independents can quickly purchase an alphabet soup of designations and hope their clients don't ask too many questions.

Vice President and other Useless Titles

While brokerage firms do not allow mail-order designations on business cards, they do hand the title of *Vice President* to almost everyone. The title may sound impressive, but it has nothing to do with investment experience, education, or knowledge. Nor does it have anything to do with client satisfaction. The title of *Vice President* is strictly a marketing designation. Clients may feel more comfortable working with an "officer" of the firm.

The title, *Vice President,* simply reflects the amount of commission generated by the advisor. The more they sell, the more prestigious the title becomes. Titles that signify a higher level of sales may include Executive Vice President, Senior Vice President, or Managing Director. A new stockbroker can become a Senior Vice President in a short time if one wealthy relative opens an account and does a lot of commission business.

Experts Lacking Knowledge

The supreme end of education is expert discernment in all things—the power to tell the good from the bad, the genuine from the counterfeit, and to prefer the good and the genuine to the bad and the counterfeit.
> —Samuel Johnson

Can you imagine a world where doctors are not required to attend medical school and lawyers do not have to go to law school? Would you hire an accountant who does not know how to read the tax code? What if your child's teacher did not finish high school and was functionally illiterate? Chances are you will not be satisfied with the results. Yet this is exactly how the investment industry operates. There are no educational requirements to enter the investment business or any needed to stay in.

Academic Background of Financial Advisors

Most people are hired in the business because they have sales skills or social status, not because they have a financial background or investment acumen. You do not even need a high school diploma to become a stockbroker or investment advisor as long as you pass a relatively simple state or federal exam.

Many investment firms run in-house sales training for new advisors, which can last several weeks. While at "boot camp" rookies familiarize themselves with the firm's products and services, and learn to make cold calls and practice other sales skills. When boot camp is over, rookies return home and start their career selling "expert" investment advice.

Over the last few years the SEC has put pressure on investment firms to provide ongoing education to brokers. The continuing education program (CE) grew out of an unprecedented number of complaints and lawsuits against stockbrokers and other advisors in the industry. While the CE requirement is a step in the right direction, it does not address the real problem. Most CE classes I attended concentrated on sales practices and legal issues in an effort to reduce the number of lawsuits. As a result, CE does very little to educate advisors on the basics of finance, economics, and portfolio management.

The CE programs are also misused. To see how far fetched the program can become, here is one real life example. A few years back, I took a college graduate course in portfolio management. Just out of curiosity, I called the compliance department at my firm to see if they would allow this course to count toward my annual CE credits. The firm would not allow the course to count because the college was not an approved CE provider. The very next week, an insurance representative was in our office and he took a group of brokers to lunch. His company was authorized to issue CE credits and if we listened to his sales pitch on annuities, we would all "earn" three credit hours.

Higher Education is a Low Priority

You don't need a fancy diploma to be successful in this business. If your clients think the market is going up, sell them stocks. If they think it's going down, sell them bonds. Just give your clients what they want and you will be successful.

—Office Manager at a Large Brokerage Firm

As professionals, you would expect investment advisors to eagerly seek advanced college degrees and professional designations. Surprisingly, there is no evidence to support that notion. I estimate less than one quarter of all brokers participate in formal education outside of their firm. Many Wall Street firms are neutral on the subject of a professional education. From management's perspective, a broker's job is to sell products and services. A detailed understanding of the markets and the economy is not essential to that job; in fact, it could hinder sales. It has been whispered to me many times, "Never let the facts get in the way of a good story."

Often a new advisor is not in a position to pursue an education, even if he wanted to. Most trainees earn a meager salary while in a training status, and they know the salary will not last. By the end of the second year, brokers are expected to support themselves on 100% commission. As a result, they spend all of their time prospecting for new clients. Recall that only 60% of new brokers make it past the three-year mark. Any thought of pursuing an academic education must take a back seat to putting food on the table.

Investment Advice and the Performance Gap

The public has little knowledge of the way Wall Street works. Large brokerage firms have hundreds of analysts covering thousands of investments, plus dozens of economists following the economic beat. This impressive network of brainpower gives many people the impression that stockbrokers and other financial advisors are very knowledgeable and offer superior advice. This is not the case.

DALBAR Study of Investor Returns

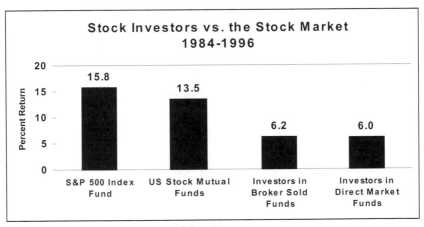

Source: DALBAR Financial Services

The fact that advisors are not well trained is evident in the DALBAR data shown above. Notice the small difference in return between investors who buy funds from brokers and those who buy direct from no-load fund companies. The results are almost identical, and well below the market. After accounting for commissions and other fees, brokerage investors likely performed below direct market no-load investors.

Conclusion

Despite the aura of advice from an "expert," the average financial advisor is no better at picking investments than is the general public. I have found that advisors fall for the same mistakes as individual investors, i.e. market timing and chasing the hot dot. This is due primarily to a lack of training on the part of advisor and the conflict of interest that exists between the sellers of investment products and the buyers. If Wall Street firms decided to train their salespeople on academic knowledge, perhaps they could be of greater assistance to their clients and begin to close the performance gap.

Obviously, the DALBAR study reflects the average advisor and the range of competence varies greatly. The challenge is being able to tell the difference between a good advisor and a bad one. Now that bankers, lawyers, accountants, and the local barber have gotten in the investment advice business, the task of finding a competent advisor has become more difficult. In any event, astute investors should research the background of a potential advisor before employing their services.

Chapter 9

The Persuasive Power of the Press

News is that which will create greatest excitement among the greatest number.

—Ayn Rand, Fountainhead

Interviewing for *Barron's*, journalist Gene Epstein asked University of Chicago economist and Noble Prize Laureate Merton Miller what advice he would give the average investor. Miller gave Epstein a surprising answer:

> "What advice would you give the average investor?"
>
> *Don't quote me on this, but I'd say don't read Barron's."*
>
> "Why?"
>
> *"Because it will only tease you about investment opportunities you'd best avoid."*
>
> Hats off to *Barron's* for printing Miller's honest answer.[53]

---

53. Gene Epstein, Prizing Caution, *Barron's*, June 2, 1997, pg. 28

How good are investment selections found in newspapers, magazines, books, investment newsletters, and the Internet? They may be entertaining and informative, but according to independent studies, they offer little value to investors seeking superior performance. In fact, most recommendations in the financial press lead to returns below the average for all investors. This chapter reviews the investment information found in the printed media and shows how the data contributes to the wide performance gap between market returns and investor performance.

Newsletters

The media, including newsletter writers, will never admit to poor performance, nor do they have to. The Security and Exchange Commission does not govern the media. Instead, they fall under the First Amendment and freedom of the press. As a result, newspapers, magazines, and other publications do not have to report the performance of their recommendations. If they do happen to publish a return, it does not have to be accurate.

In 1985 the US Supreme Court ruled that *investment newsletters* were exempt from the Investment Advisors Act of 1940 and therefore not subject to SEC regulation. The courts view newsletters as *journalistic articles,* not investment advice. As a result, newsletter writers can claim they achieved any performance they wish, even if it is not true, and their claim is protected under the First Amendment.

A perfect example of this is the *California Technology Stock Letter,* published by Michael Murphy. In a recent advertisement for this newsletter Murphy claimed incredible stock-picking ability, routinely touting stocks that had 700% to 900% returns. Unfortunately, Murphy must not be taking his own advice. The Monterey Murphy New World Technology Fund, personally managed by Mr. Murphy, was the *worst* performing technology fund in the country over a three-year period ending in 1998. The performance of this high flying wonder was *negative* 8.3% annualized, compared with a 27.6% annual gain during the same period for the average tech-fund fund.[54]

Michael Murphy is not alone. In 1987 Joe Granville predicted the market would crash and became famous when it did. While Granville was correct on that occasion, he has been wrong ever since. Although Granville claims high returns, for an 18 year period ending in 1998, *The Granville Market Letter* lost 22.5%. Despite this dismal record, the news media still seek his insight, and he is hailed as an important market guru.

As a group, newsletter writers have a terrible track record of picking stocks and mutual funds. *The Hulbert Financial Digest* has been tracking the performance of investment newsletters since 1980. During the past fifteen years, Mark Hulbert found that only two newsletters that have beaten the Wilshire 5000 (a measure of the broad US market).[55] Since most letters engaged in some sort of market timing, the average letter had only 54% invested in equities during the period. That hurts performance in a bull market. Regardless of that fact, almost every "stock only" letter failed to keep pace with the general market average.

One newsletter that did perform well in Hulbert's study was the *Value Line Investment Survey.* Each week *Value Line* evaluates 1,700 stocks and awards 100 of them with the top "timeliness" ranking. A portfolio of these top 100 stocks would have beaten the market handily since the early 1980s. Unfortunately, the Value

---

54. Karen Damato, "A Tech Expert's Own Fund Takes Worst Place," *The Wall Street Journal*, 2/26/99, c1
55. Mark Hulbert, "Newsletters vs. Funds: Which are the Better Performers?" *AAII Journal,* September 1998

Line Fund, which is managed using the timeliness rankings, had no such luck. The Value Line Fund returned 2.0% *less* than the market over the same period of time. This is a very important point. In theory, the Value Line system works, but in practice it does not. The difference between the two is trading costs and human judgement. The "real world" weakness that applies to Value Line data applies to other strategies as well. It is always possible to beat the market in theory but it is much harder in practice.

Magazines

Warren Buffett once said, "Wall Street is a place where people who ride a limo to work get their investment advice from people who ride the subway." Taken one step further, those people riding in limos may be reading an investment magazine written by a journalist who cannot *afford* the subway.

Finance magazines have become one of the most influential sources of information for do-it-yourself investors as these publications have grown in both circulation and number. Over the years there has also been a major editorial change. Prior to 1990, financial magazine articles were generally aimed at helping readers cope with financial planning issues, as well as helping them understand the workings of the markets. In recent years, the publications have focused efforts on providing readers with specific investment advice. While this may have led to wider readership, it has *not* resulted to higher financial returns for readers.

Money Magazine Study

Money magazine has recommended specific stocks since the early 1980s. Many of these recommendations occur in the annual *Forecast* issue published in late

December. In this special issue, *Money* attempts to make sweeping forecasts about the markets, highlighting stocks the editors think offer superior potential in the coming year. *Money* editors also made specific sell recommendations in most *Forecast* issues.

Since *Money* is a favorite magazine of do-it-yourself investors, major advertisers tend to be no-load mutual fund companies and discount brokerage firms. Full-service brokerage firms like Merrill Lynch and Salomon Smith Barney are not big advertisers in *Money*, and as a result the editors have no remorse about smearing them in favor of larger clients. In 1995, Smith Barney grew tired of the name calling and used the annual *Forecast* issue to show how poor *Money* editors were at selecting stocks.

Performance Results of Stock in *Money* Magazine's Annual Forecast Issue

| | Recommendations | | S&P 500 |
	Buy	Sell	
1990	-16.7%	-23.1%	-3.2%
1991	38.3%	23.4%	30.6%
1992	-13.1%	83.6%	7.7%
1993	-5.8%	12.0%	10.0%
1994	2.1%	NA	1.3%
Annual	-0.8%	18.2%	8.7%
Cumulative	-3.7%	95.1%	51.7%

Source: Salomon Smith Barney (SSB) Consulting Group

*Money did not make sell recommendations in 1994.

During the five-year period, *Money's* buy recommendations were far below the stock market. In fact, the cumulative buy recommendations lost 3.7% over the period while the S&P 500 *gained* 51.7%. More interesting was *Money's* sell recommendations. If you had *bought* the stocks that *Money* advised you to sell, you would have beaten the stock market by a whopping 43% percent!

Forbes' Honor Roll

Many investors rely on published rankings to select their mutual funds. Each year *Forbes* magazine publishes an "Honor Roll" of mutual funds, highlighting those the editors believe will provide steady, long-term performance in both bull and bear markets. *Forbes* claims these funds have "consistency of performance and toughness in tough times."[56]

Princeton University professor Burton Malkeil, author of the widely acclaimed investment book, *A Random Walk Down Wall Street*, questioned Forbes' ability to choose mutual funds that achieve superior returns. Malkeil conducted an independent study of the Honor Roll funds and found that they resulted in returns consistently below the market.[57]

For the fifteen years between 1975 and 1990, the Honor Roll funds underperformed the S&P 500 by a mere 1.4%. However, in the later years of this period the funds were significantly below average. From 1983 to 1990 the Honor Roll Funds returned 6.0% below the market, and the group did not beat the market in *any* one year. Other studies of the *Forbes* Honor Roll support Malkeil's conclusion.

---

56. *Forbes*, August 29, 1994, pg. 132
57. Burton G. Malkeil, *A Random Walk Down Wall Street,* W.W. Norton & Co. NY, 1996, pg. 444

Gauging the Market with Magazine Covers

Let's imagine for a moment that you have been on an extended trip to a remote region of the world. For three years you have had been completely cut off from business news and have no idea what has happened to the stock market. Upon your arrival back in the US, you notice the cover on a popular business magazine. It reads, "Market Collapse May Send Economy Into Tailspin," and a second reads "Armageddon?"

Uh-oh. Before leaving home you had put your entire retirement account into a stock mutual fund. Are you wiped out? No. A quick call to the fund company reveals that the value of your account has *doubled* over the past three years. You wonder what "market" the magazines are talking about.

Magazine covers convey how editors believe we all feel about the markets *today,* not by what will happen over the long run or in the distant future. If stocks go up, magazines print pictures of bulls and dollar bills. If stocks go down, bears cover the newsstand. In 1991 Ned Davis elaborated on this subject in his colorful book, *Being Right or Making Money.*[58] He reviewed magazine covers before and after major turning points in the markets. Davis found the covers are a good way to determine when crowd psychology is at an extreme. When a large number of covers are bullish or bearish, investors should wait thirty days, then buy and sell against the trend. Davis says this method has proved to be an accurate indicator of future trends nearly 80% of the time. Here are some examples in his book:

On January 1, 1973, *Barron's* headlines read "Not a Bear Among Them," referring to the

---

58. Ned Davis, *Being Right or Making Money*, published by the author, fourth printing 1995, pg. 39

panel of investment experts on Barron's Roundtable. The article said the panel was "bullish on Wall Street, business, and the markets." Over the next 30 days, the worst bear market since 1929 began. In 1973 and 1974 the S&P 500 fell over 40%, and small stocks fell over 80%.

August 1979, after six years of poor stock market performance, *Business Week* announced "The Death of Equities" on their cover. They advised readers to sell stocks and invest in bonds linked to the price of gold and oil. That issue marked the beginning of a major a rally on Wall Street and the peak in gold and oil prices.

In early October 1987, *Fortune* magazine printed a cover story titled "Why Greenspan is Bullish." The story praised the US economy as well as the stock market. Two weeks later the October '87 crash occurred and stocks lost 20% in one day.

In the scramble for readers' attention, editors capitalize on current investment sentiment to make their recommendations. Although magazines do not track their predictions, some academics do, and the results are dismal. The truth is that magazine publishers are not in the business of making readers rich by correctly predicting the market. Their job is to sell magazines and advertising. They know that stories that play on the natural fears and greed of people will increase readership and that this leads to a healthier revenue stream for the publication. The same is true of newspapers.

Newspapers

Most newspapers publish stock and bond market information on a regular basis. When the stock market makes a large move, journalists try to find the reason why. They may get their information from the national wire service, following up with a telephone call to a couple of local experts for a quote. As a result, the reason the stock market did this or that can be very different depending on the paper you read. The reason the market moved as published in the *Boston Globe* may differ from the *Chicago Sun*, which may differ again from the *Los Angeles Times*. It's really up to the reporter covering the story, and the opinion of the local "experts" they interview.

Newspapers and Their Advertising Clients

Some investment companies spend a lot of money advertising in newspapers across the country. On occasion, when an expert is needed, a journalist will call on the newspaper's advertising clients for their comments on the markets. These comments are then fed into the news story. Though much of this name-dropping is subtle, there have been obvious attempts to steer readers toward companies who purchase ad space from the paper.

Investors Business Daily (IBD) ran a front-page article on December 31, 1996 about investment opportunities in *sector funds*. The story was titled "Playing Hot Sectors with Mutual Funds." Fidelity Select sector funds were mentioned several times in the article. While the story was not out of the ordinary, the full-page ad for Fidelity Select funds printed on page three was obvious. In rereading the article, it became clear that the story was planted by IBD in conjunction with the ad for Fidelity funds. The author mentioned Fidelity five times in the article, and barely mentioned companies that offer competing funds.

On August 4, 1998, technical analyst Ralph Acampora from Prudential Securities made a bearish call on the stock market. He made his announcement on national TV about two in the afternoon, after the market had fallen substantially earlier in the day. The following morning, *USA Today* carried a lead story about the sell-off, highlighting Acampora's comments and featuring a picture of him on the front page of the business section. Acampora was *USA Today's* master of the stock market.

The whole hype job struck me as strange. Why all the attention? About half way through the sports section I got my answer. On page C12 there was a full-page ad for Prudential Securities. The ad said, "When Your Goal is Capital Preservation, Call Prudential." Now it made sense. In exchange for hyping Acampora, Prudential bought a full-page ad in the newspaper. It was a well-planned media blitz.

Acampora was wrong about the market this time. Within a year the Dow Jones Industrial Average was up over 40%, and it surged through 10,000 for the first time. *USA Today* didn't print that story.

Stock Advice and Newspapers

Newspapers are not held accountable for their investment recommendations, nor do they keep track of the results. *USA Today* frequently picks stocks in their "Market Highlights" section. These stocks are based on analysts' recommendations from various brokerage firms that happen to advertise in the newspaper. M. Mark Walker and Gay B. Hatfield of the University of Mississippi evaluated the performance of these stock picks to see if investors could achieve above-average returns by following them.[59]

The study covered a period from 1988 to 1990 and looked at 329 recommendations. Walker and Gay found that the stocks only led to superior returns if an investor knew the names of recommended stocks *before* the newspaper was published. If investors bought the stocks *after* the paper was published, they would have realized below market returns. Of course, acting on inside information is illegal, so the first part of the study is mute. The moral of the story is that the newspapers do not provide investment information that the average person can use to make superior decisions.

Hypothetical Strategies and Real Returns

William O'Neil is a big name in investment research. The William O'Neil Company publishes *Investors Business Daily* and offers wide assortment of investment publications. O'Neil also runs seminars based on his proprietary C-A-N-S-L-I-M method of stock selection. His technique of choosing growth stocks is based on years of study using past market winners as examples. The O'Neil method is well researched and theoretically accurate. However, it has failed to produce superior returns when real money is applied.

David Ryan, Vice President and portfolio manager at the William O'Neil Company became famous by winning a stock-picking contest run by Stanford University in the mid-1980s. His track record over three years was an incredible 1,397%. Unfortunately for Ryan this was only a theoretical gain. Actual money was not used in the contest.[60]

59. M. Mark Walker and Gay B. Hatfield, "Professional Stock Recommendations: Implications for Individual Investors," *Financial Services Review*, vol. 5, no. 1 (1996), pg. 13-29

In 1993, Ryan became the portfolio manager of the New USA Growth Fund. The fund used the O'Neil C-A-N-S-L-I-M method of stock selection as well as Ryan's obvious stock picking ability. After three years of trying, Ryan failed to come close to the theoretical results of the Stanford contest or to the market average. Management expenses were high, and portfolio turnover averaged 500% per year, which resulted in large trading costs. In early 1997 the New USA Growth Fund was sold to another company, and the assets were merged into a more successful fund. Ryan stayed on with the William O'Neil Company.

The failure of the New USA Growth Funds is an example of how difficult it is to take a strategy that works on paper and make it work with real money. With the proliferation of investment software and the availability of detailed financial information, anyone with a computer can develop strategies that would have worked well in the past. However, there is no guarantee the strategy will work in the future. Orders with real money change the nature of the market in a way that no model can accurately predict. As a result, actual returns are never the same as expected returns, regardless of the time and effort put into the strategy.

Books

Investment books can be categorized into three broad types. The first type of book is written for academics and can be found on college bookshelves. The second type is written for the general reader who is interested in improving their investment skill. The third type seems to be written to make the author rich at the expense of the reader.

---

60. Jack D. Schwager, *Market Wizards*, HarperBusiness, 1989, pg. 238

Books for General Reading

Many titles for general reading have wide reader acceptance like *Bogle on Mutual Funds* by John Bogle, Chairman of the Vanguard Group, and *Investment Biker* by Jim Rogers. These books are written for a wide audience, attempting to capture the interest of professional and non-professional investors. Experienced money managers like Bogle and Rogers make excellent reading. The authors are original, honest, and have something genuine to say. There are times when money managers can go a little overboard. Peter Lynch, former manager of the Fidelity Magellan Fund, wrote three books on beating the stock market. While they were fine books, they did little to improve the results of the average reader.

Some books for general reading on financial topics are written by journalists. Typically, these works are well researched and very informative. *Fidelity's World* by Diana B. Henriques offers a behind-the-scenes look at the mutual fund business. *Buffett: The Making of an American Capitalist* by Roger Lowenstien is an excellent journalistic work about the life of Warren Buffett. *The Confidence Game* by Steven Solomon explains in detail the thinking of Federal Reserve Chairman Greenspan. These books offer wonderful insight into special topics within the financial services industry.

Make-Me-Rich Books

Unfortunately, many books are published for the purpose of making the author rich, not the reader. These are "get rich quick" books. Here you will find every gimmick imaginable, from heavenly advice found in Wade Cook's *The Stock Market Miracle*, to astrology readings in *Investing by the Stars*. There are books that appeal to pure greed, like *The Investor's Guide for Making Megabucks on Mergers*, and *Midas Investing: How You*

Can Make at Least 20% in the Market this Year and Every Year.

Get-rich-quick books tend to follow media events. The real estate boom in the late 1970s and early 1980s brought on a rash of real estate speculation books. My favorite was *Nothing Down*—a book on how to make a fortune ripping off desperate home sellers. In the late 1980s the Japanese economy was booming, which resulted in books like *Japanese Stocks: A Basic Guide for Intelligent Investors,* and *The Japanese Miracle.* Years ago these books were required reading; now they sell for a nickel at garage sales across the country. None of these strategies stood a chance of working.

Mutual fund investing has seen tremendous growth in the 1990s. Naturally, there are several books on how to pick the best mutual funds. One popular book, *The Best 100 Mutual Funds You Can Buy,* is a classic example. Every year self-proclaimed investment expert Gordon K. Williamson tells us which mutual funds to buy. Although, his *Best 100 Funds* book does not discuss past performance, I compared Williamson's 1994 fund picks in two important categories for a closer look at his predictive skills.

The "BEST" Funds vs. Lipper Averages
July 1994 – July 1997

	Growth Funds	Growth and Income
The "BEST" funds	22.9%	20.6%
Lipper Average for Category	23.1%	23.4%
Wilshire 5000 Index	26.7%	26.7%

Overall, Williamson's picks performed below average against the Lipper benchmark and significantly below the market average. Of the 25 funds in the study, only two performed better than the Wilshire 5000 Index. In the back of his book, Williamson boasts he is one of the most *highly trained investment counselors in the United States.* If this self-proclaimed god of investing cannot pick winning funds, how can we mere mortals hope to succeed?

The New Media–Chat Rooms and the Internet

"Peer into my computer screen, and let us see what the future holds."

Crystal balls have always fascinated mankind. Soothsayers throughout history have made bold predictions of fame and fortune by peering into the glowing light of a crystal ball. In the modern world, computer monitors have replaced crystal balls, and Internet chat rooms have replaced spirits of the deep.

Data Services and Analysis Programs

Watching lights blink on a computer screen and looking at stock charts all day may tell you exactly what happened in the past, but they do little to predict the future. A high-speed computer will not increase your investment knowledge or performance, although it may give you a tax deduction. Flashy investment software programs do nothing new to enhance returns; they simply receive data faster and crunch more numbers. Read the *Theory of Investment Value,* written by William Burr in 1936, and you will discover that basic investment techniques have not changed in fifty years; only the speed of making calculations has changed.

Contrary to claims in advertisements, investment programs do not enlighten the user with special information. It is true that data can be obtained almost instantaneously, but data are not a substitute for real understanding. If you don't know what you are looking at or how to analyze to the information, the data are useless. With all the computing power at hand, most mutual fund managers have not been able to beat the basic market averages over the years.

Fools One and All

Internet investing is all the rage. There are thousands of investing web sites on the Internet. Some offer quotes, charts, graphs and a variety of other services. Others sites push investment products, new issues, or whatever. One popular site is the Motley Fool. It was started by a couple of college kids in the early 1990s. Just about everything you ever wanted to know about the markets can be found here, except clues to superior investment returns.

One service the Motley Fool provides is model portfolios of stocks designed to beat the stock market. Mark Hulbert, editor of the *Hulbert Financial Digest,* monitored the performance of Motley Fool's model stock portfolios over the years. For three years ending in 1997, the results are not impressive. Hulbert found most Fool portfolios lagged the stock market, and one lost a huge amount. As rule, the Motley Fool will discontinue a portfolio if it underperforms after a year or so. One defunct portfolio lost over 50% before it was discontinued.

The Fool is not required to report performance in accordance with industry standards, since they are not a registered investment advisor. However, they do try to maintain objectivity. One of the portfolios, the Motley Fool #2, did beat the market by a wide margin during the period. The portfolio contained two hot technology stocks, which accounted for most of the gain.

Fraud on the Web

Many web sites offer investors the opportunity to swap ideas in an open forum called an Internet chat room. It has been my experience that a chat room is a place where you can have a totally useless conversation about investing with someone who knows very little about the markets, but is convinced he knows everything.

Chat rooms are also crawling with fraud. Stock operators try to manipulate prices by creating rumors and hyping stock. In early 1999 E-mail complaints to the SEC alleging Internet stock frauds were up to 300 a day, according to the General Accounting Office. Claims range from simple pump-and-dump schemes[61] to sophisticated ploys such as counterfeit brokerage Web sites. Unfortunately, the SEC has not been able to keep up with the situation, and fraudulent claims flourish. To further complicate matters, the SEC has recently lost more than 40% of their enforcement staffers in important markets like New York and San Francisco.

More and more inexperienced investors are being lured into the Web. Hundreds of thousands of people have opened Internet trading accounts under the false belief that it will lead to easy riches. If achieving superior returns was easy as buying a computer and trading on tips from chat rooms, we would all be rich. In reality, there is much higher probability you will be lulled into a stock manipulation scheme that will cost you a lot of money. A computer is a great tool, but common sense goes a lot further than a super-powered Intel processor.

---

61. A pump-and-dump scheme involves a stock promoter who quietly buys a large quantity of a company's stock and then launches a huge media blitz about the company, pushing the stock price up. If the price gets high enough, the promoter sells the stock for a large profit. This is illegal stock manipulation.

Summary

Newspapers, newsletters, magazines and other members of the print media typically sensationalize their information in an effort to hold readers' attention and attract new readers. The investment ideas typically encourage *chasing the hot dot* and *market timing behavior*, which results in the wide performance gap between the markets return and investor performance.

The printing press is a powerful tool. It can save lives and start wars, but it cannot tell you which mutual fund will beat the market next year. Following specific investment advice from a mass media source is generally not a good idea. Although the information seems important and relevant, unless you have a broad perspective and a deep understanding of the subject, it can do you more harm than good.

Individual investors spend hundreds of millions of dollars each year on investment information. Money spent buying newsletters, newspapers, and magazines would be put to better use if invested in good quality bonds or stock *index funds*. As Merton Miller stated in Barron's, the media will *only tease you about investment opportunities you had best avoid.*

Chapter 10

Mutual Fund Follies

The illusions of hope are apt to close one's eyes to the painful truth.

—Harry F. Banks

The mutual fund industry is a tremendous success story. It has grown from a few hundred funds twenty years ago to over ten thousand today. The number of mutual fund companies has also mushroomed. There are over five hundred fund companies offering almost every investment style imaginable. Mutual funds have become a household word and are the investment of choice for many people. Over forty million Americans have an interest in at least one mutual fund, and assets in those funds total almost five trillion dollars.

Mutual Fund Growth

Mutual fund companies compete in a fiercely competitive industry. As a result, they must develop funds that attract the attention of advisors and the general public. This is accomplished by having one or more funds "beat" the market during the year. The best way to increase the odds of having a winning fund is to have a many funds. In order to hedge their bets, most fund companies carry ten or more funds and continually introduce new funds each year. From 1985 to 1995, the average number of funds per family nearly doubled from six to ten.[62]

Mutual Fund Proliferation

Year	Number of Mutual Fund Companies	Number of Mutual Funds	Funds per Company
1985	252	1,528	6.0
1990	423	2,917	6.9
1995	558	5,761	10.3

Source: The Investment Company Institute

As you can see from the table below, a fund family with ten funds has a much greater probability of having at least one winning fund. Fidelity has become the premier mutual fund supermarket. With over 100 funds, they expect to have several funds to boast about each year.

Probability of Beating a Benchmark

Number of Funds in the Family	Probability of at Least One Fund Beating the Market	Probability of at Least Three Funds Beating the Market
3	75%	5%
6	90%	50%
10	95%	75%

Source:Richard M. Ennis, CFA

62. Richard M. Ennis, "The Structure of the Investment Management Industry; Revisiting the New Paradigm," *Financial Analysts Journal*, July/August 1997, pg. 6-13

Creating a New Fund

Ideas for new funds come from a variety of sources. Some come from portfolio managers and securities analysts; others come from the marketing department. While it is noble to think that fund companies come up with their own original ideas for funds, I believe that is more the exception than the rule. The fastest way to bring in money is to throw together a hot new fund based on a hot sector in the market. Ned Johnson, former president of Fidelity Investments, said if the public would buy a fund, he would create it, though he himself would not put *one nickel* of his own money in it.[63] If one day the public decided chicken farms were a good investment, five or six chicken farm funds would quickly be created by the mutual fund industry.

Some new funds are really not new at all. They are reworked old funds that have been laggards in the family and needed a facelift. A fund may be reintroduced with a zippy new name, an energetic portfolio manager, and new marketing blitz. It is less expensive to try to save an old fund that already has assets than it is to start a new one from scratch.

Me-Too Funds

Most fund companies have limited resources to research new ideas, and the chance of discovering a new winning strategy is remote. Time is better spent selling funds than trying to create superior investment strategies. As a result, most fund companies simply copy hot selling ideas in the marketplace. If one fund company offers a popular new fund, it will not be long before dozens of "me-too" funds are born.

---

63. Diane B. Henriques, *Fidelities World,* Scribner, NY, 1995, pg. 234. Quoted during an interview with former Fidelity money manager Mark Shenkman.

While working as a broker, I was able to gauge the strength of the market by the number of me-too funds created. When it seemed like every mutual fund wholesaler was pushing a particular style of fund, the style was usually close to its own market peak. In late 1997, Real Estate Investment (REIT) funds were very popular. After two years of robust gains in the REIT market, almost every fund company had a new or improved REIT fund. Just like clockwork, during the 12-month period that followed, REIT funds were one of the worst performing categories. In the first half of 1999, nearly every fund company was touting its growth fund, which was loaded with high-tech stocks. Was this a sign that growth and high-tech may be peaking and that stodgy old value stocks may soon outperform? As of this writing value stocks have outperformed growth stocks by a wide margin in 1999.

Buying a Rising Star

Mutual fund managers are frequently quoted in major publications such as *The Wall Street Journal* and *Barron's*. They also appear on TV programs like Wall Street Week and CNN. The more a manager is exposed to the public, the greater following he gathers. Some fund managers become outright celebrities. The mere mention of their name adds credibility to an investment and can make or break a fund company. These are "star" managers, and their name alone is worth millions to a fund company.

When a fund manager becomes a star, the company he or she works for typically exploits the opportunity by making them *Senior Portfolio Strategist* over several funds, including many new ones. Actually, the real title should be *Senior Marketing Person.* The star manager's job is not to run the portfolios on a day to day basis, but to get in the public eye and promote their firm. Stars may be consulted on some portfolio management issues when they happen to be around, but other people make most of the decisions.

Mark Mobius of Franklin Templeton is emerging as a superstar market manager. Between 1993 and 1995 Mobius was named senior advisor of five new funds. Although Mobius has overall responsibility for the funds, he does not manage them on a day-to-day basis. He spends a lot of time going around the world speaking to brokers and investors about the virtues of investing in Templeton funds.

Star managers can also be the source of embarrassment. In early 1990 Jeff Vinick caused quite a stir at Fidelity while managing the mammoth Magellan Fund. He was caught *pumping and dumping* the stock of Motorola. After touting the stock in the press, he dumped shares during the rally that resulted from his comments. As a result of this blunder, Fidelity managers generally no longer comment on the stocks in their portfolios.

Many fund companies recruit star managers from the competition. If a fund manager jumps ship, he or she typically takes a number of their clients along. The star manager is in a good position to negotiate stock options, signing bonuses, and other perks.

Change the Name to Protect the Guilty

What did one investment company do with a tired old fund that had been performing poorly for years? It changed the name and reintroduced the fund as a top performer. After several years of mediocre performance, the Smith Barney Strategic Investor Fund was losing market share. Then an astute employee noticed that the performance, though weak, would have earned it the Number 1 spot as a social awareness fund. The only problem was the fund was not managed with a social awareness strategy. No problem!

After filing with the SEC, the Strategic Investor Fund was renamed the Concert Social Awareness Fund, and the performance was carried over from the old fund. By changing styles, the fund went from a mediocre general equity fund, to the top-performing social awareness fund in the country. The only indication of this switch was an ambiguous statement buried in the prospectus that read:

> The financial information set out below represents the financial history of the Fund prior to implementing the social awareness criteria and the Fund's performance may have been different if it had pursued a social awareness criteria since its inception.

In other words, if the fund had been managed from inception as a social awareness fund, there is no telling what the performance would have been. The SEC must have been sleeping the day Smith Barney slipped this one by.

Incubator Funds

If at first you don't succeed, destroy all evidence that you tried.

—Anonymous

When a funds company wants to try a new strategy its managers often test it on a small, private account first. If the strategy is successful, they may open the account to the public as mutual fund; if not, the account will likely be closed. These private accounts are called *incubator funds,* and a fund company may have several eggs in the incubator at a time.

If an incubator strategy is successful and the account is converted to a mutual fund, the SEC *allows* the past performance as a private account to carry forward. This is how a brand-new fund can advertise a fantastic long-term performance record even though the fund was not open to the public. While the SEC requires fair disclosure of these facts, few individual investors read the fine print. It is a clear case of legal fraud.

In 1996 the performance of the State Street Aurora Fund was over 56%, earning it the Number One spot among 407 small-cap value funds, according to Morningstar. Aurora also beat the Russell 2000 small stock index by a whopping 40% that year. Unfortunately, the fund was only open to State Street employees. No public investor could buy in. By the time Aurora opened to the public in 1997, it only had $1.2 million invested in it. Investors were attracted to the fund like a magnet and began pouring money in. Within a few months the fund held over $200 million in assets. Inflow of cash can be a turning point in the fund's style. In 1998 Aurora significantly under-performed their benchmark.

I disagree with the SEC's decision to allow mutual fund companies to use the performance of private accounts as the hypothetical performance of a mutual fund that never existed. There are huge operational differences between managing a million-dollar private account and managing a two hundred million-dollar mutual fund. If a mutual fund company must resort to advertising incubator funds to attract new capital, that does not say much for their ability to manage existing assets.

Other Marketing Claims

Mutual funds companies go to great lengths to create brand names in a mostly homogeneous industry. With the exception of the worst funds with the highest fees, the performance of most funds in a particular category can be expected to fall within a narrow range of returns over the long term. It has to be this way. There is only a finite selection of stocks to choose from. Nevertheless, fund companies will say just about anything to stand out from the pack.

Experienced Portfolio Managers Are Not Better Managers

Some mutual fund companies try to sell the age and experience of their portfolio managers. The idea is to sell the concept that older is wiser, and experienced managers are better stock pickers than younger managers. There is no academic evidence to support this claim. To the contrary, the evidence suggests that older fund managers cannot keep pace with younger managers. One recent study measured manager performance based on race, sex, age, college attended, SAT scores, MBA or non-MBA degreed, and a variety of other factors. The study concluded that young managers perform better than older ones. The researchers speculated that younger managers worked longer hours, used technology more effectively, and took more risks.[64] A screen of large-cap funds in the Morningstar Principia database reveals that managers with more than ten years tenure at a fund generally had the worst performance in the category.

Bigger Mutual Funds Are Not Better Funds

"You can't get hurt in a big game," or so the saying goes. Many large mutual funds promote their funds as solid bedrock performers, able to withstand the worst bear market. This is a marketing myth.

Big funds can have big problems. A comparison of risks and returns of the ten largest US stock funds,

---

64. Judith Chevalier and Glenn Ellison, "Are Some Mutual Fund Managers Better Than Others? Cross-Sectional Patters in Behavior and Performance," May 1998

excluding the Vanguard Index 500 fund, shows that they do not perform any better than the average mutual fund according to Lipper. About half the large funds were below the Lipper Average and half were above it. Only one large fund beat the performance of the Vanguard Index 500 Fund, and that was by only 0.10%. Large funds are not better, just bigger.

"Bigger is better" may have validity in one respect. Due to the amount of money in a large fund it must hold many of the same stocks as the S&P 500; therefore it should perform close to the market's return. There should not be a time when a large fund grossly under-performs or outperforms the market average. Large funds become large because some portfolio manager at some point in the life of the fund achieved superior returns. But the top performance will not likely occur again. Today shareholders can expect performance fairly close to the market's returns less operating fees and other expenses.

In the End it is Regression to the Mean

There are about 5,700 stock funds to select from today. This is interesting since only about a thousand or so stocks are large enough to be included in most of those funds. That means many funds hold the same stocks, and consequently, perform similarly over time. This phenomenon is called *regression to the mean.*

The regression tendency of mutual funds can be shown with a study of the Morningstar Principia database (see the graph on the next page.) Screening the data for large-cap mutual funds with 15-year track records turns up about 150 names. Year after year the average yearly variation between funds is about 6.0%. However, over a 15-year period, the variation falls to 1.7%. As the time horizon increases, regression to the mean in all categories begins to occur. Most of the variation in long-term performance can be explained by operating expenses and trading costs, not by a funds style or the skill of the manager.

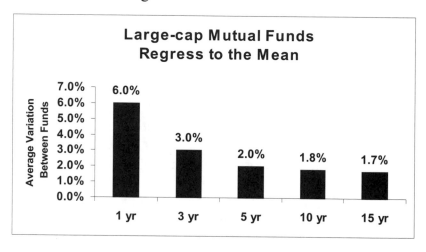

Part II and the Performance Gap

Part II of this book explored a number of conflicts that exist between the sellers of investment products and the buyers. We could fill ten volumes on this subject and still not hit all the sales gimmicks used in the investment industry, but there is little point in doing that. The fact is that Wall Street encourages people to invest in a manner that *causes* a performance gap. Remember that the industry exists to make money from you, not for you. There is nothing wrong with paying for investment products and advice, as long as *your* best interests are at hand. *Caveat emptor*; let the buyer beware.

PART III

Closing the Performance Gap

Chapter 11

Solutions & Expectations

We should never trust an answer less simple than the one that will do the job perfectly well.

—William of Ockham

In Part I of this book we discovered the huge performance gap that exists between financial market returns and individual investors in the markets. We found several reasons for the performance gap including high costs, market timing behavior, and chasing hot investments. The financial industry presents ideas to the public in a manner that makes people believe they can beat the markets. Part II examined the pitfalls of following the recommendations of investment "experts" and trying to beat the street.

Part III is about closing the performance gap. We will learn how to achieve a fair return on your money without taking undue risks. By avoiding high fees, market timing, and investment choices based on past performance, you can enjoy the fruits of the marketplace. There is another lesson to learn in this section. The power of tax efficiency can significantly increase your wealth over the years.

What You Can Reasonably Expect from this Strategy

The last fifteen years have spoiled us. The stock and bond markets have returned unprecedented gains in the 80s and 90s. Many investors believe the incredible bull market will continue for many years into the future. A 1999 survey of investors conducted by PaineWebber found that the average person believes the stock market will achieve annual returns of over 15% for the next ten years.[65] Obviously, most investors have not experienced a prolonged bear market, but that does not mean they will not occur in the future. Before we jump into specifics about investing in the markets, a review of past returns and future expectations is warranted.

Contrary to recent history, there have been long periods of time when the stock market was not a great investment. From 1968 though 1982, the stock market returned 6.3% and long-term government bonds 2.9%. More important, inflation was 7.3% during the period, meaning real returns for stocks and bonds were negative. It was a terrible fifteen years for owners of financial assets. Contrast that with the 1984 though 1998 period. Stocks returned 17.9% and government bonds 12.2% at a time when inflation was only 3.3%, meaning the markets generated unprecedented *real* gains.

Twice in the twentieth century there were wide swings in value of financial assets. The bull-bear market cycle seems to take about thirty years to complete. Basically, every generation has had a bull market and a bear market. The baby boomers have not seen a bear market. Know one knows when the down cycle will be or what will cause it. But it is very likely to occur in the next twenty years.

65. PaineWebber's Index of Investor Optmism, *Business Investors Daily,* April 28, 1999, pg. b1

Inflation Adjusted Returns

We invest in stocks because over long periods of time, stocks perform better than bonds and money funds, but how much can we expect in the future? That question cannot be answered only by looking at the returns in the past because inflation distorts returns. If an investment generated a nominal return of 5.0% and at the same time inflation was 5.0%, the *real* return was 0.0% (before paying taxes on full 5.0% gain). The best way to state the returns of stocks and bonds is as some percent over inflation. Since 1926, large US stocks returned about 8.0% over inflation and bonds about 3.0% over inflation. Treasury bills average less than 1.0% over inflation.[66] The recent strength in the US economy and the structure of the stock index has caused an upward distortion in the number. For planning purposes, investors should use an inflation-adjusted return for stocks of about 6.0%.

If we apply these long-term figures to today's inflation rate of 2.0%, it leads me to believe that large US stocks should return about 8.0% over the next thirty years, and bonds should return close to 5.0%. An 8.0% expected return from stocks is much lower than the 15% return investors expect according to the PaineWebber survey. Once again, this estimate is based on long-term results while most investors are only looking at recent history.

---

66. Ibbotson Associates, *Stocks, Bonds, Bill and Inflation, 1999 Yearbook,* Chicago, Illinois

Historical Returns and Future Estimates of Stocks, Bonds, and Inflation

	1926-1998	Estimate 2000-2030
Inflation Rate	3%	2%
Bond Returns (nominal)	6%	5%
Bonds—Inflation adjusted	3%	3%
Stock Returns (nominal)	11%	8%
Stocks – Inflation adjusted	8%	6%

The figures above are before commissions, fees, and income tax, therefore should not be confused with the returns individual investors will achieve. It is very likely that the returns of the average investor will be much lower due to costs. Astute investors know that in the long term, it is important to keep fees low and reduce taxable income.

My estimates of future market returns are less than what the sellers of investment products like to infer. Many advisors will quote an expected return on stocks of 11% or higher because that is the true historic number, but this is flawed thinking. It does not take into consideration the historic inflation rate of 3.1% or the recent trend in inflation expectations. Expectations of return should move *lower* as the markets move higher and inflation subsides. Much of the bull market in stocks and bonds during the 1980s and 1990s was a direct result of inflation falling from 13% in 1980 to less than 2.0% in 1999.

Assets that produce income are worth more when inflation drops. This means earnings from corporations are worth more in a low-inflation environment. The more investors pay for those earnings, the *lower* their total return will be from that point on. A corporate earnings stream can be compared to bond interest. Bonds pay a certain interest rate each year, but the total return you get from the bond is based on the price you pay. The more you pay for the right to the interest stream, the *lower* your total return on the bond. The same mechanisms are at work in the stock market. The more you pay for future earnings, the *lower* your total return on stocks in the future.

There is another reason to embrace a conservative stance for expected stock and bond returns. As part of a retirement savings strategy, you should create an investment plan (see chapter 14). The plan will require that you make an estimate of your investment return over the years. It is far wiser to use a conservative estimate of return and be pleasantly surprised if the market performs well than to use a high number and watch the market perform poorly. In the second scenario you may not accumulate enough money to retire.

Overview of Part III

Chapter 12—Investing in the Stock Market

Almost every financial plan will undoubtedly lead to some investment in the stock market. What is the best way to achieve a fair return in stocks? The answer is to develop a diversified portfolio of low-cost, market-matching *index funds*. Indexing the stock markets make a lot of sense for four reasons. First, index funds are low cost; second, they perform better than almost all active strategies; third, they reduce the desire to chase the hot dot since you already own the stocks that are performing well; and fourth, they are tax efficient.

Nearly every academic study concludes that index funds offer better performance overall than active (beat the market) strategies. Few active managers are able to achieve the returns of indexes, let allow beat them—and it is impossible to tell which managers will be successful in the future. *The markets make people wealthy, not speculative strategies designed to beat the markets.*

Chapter 13—Investing in the Bond Market

This chapter gives the reader insight into the bond market and outlines two strategies to keep costs low. One strategy calls for investing in high quality, individual short-term bonds which avoids the expense of investing in mutual funds. Generally, a self-managed bond portfolio generates a higher return than a fund, especially in the area of tax-free bonds. Individual bonds can be purchased from a variety of sources. You may purchase US Treasury bonds directly from the government or through any stockbroker. The concept of developing and maintaining a bond "ladder" is also discussed in this chapter.

The second strategy concerns bond index funds and building a portfolio based on these funds. When considering high-yield bonds or other complex fixed-income assets, I recommend using index funds instead of individual bonds.

Chapter 14—Financial Goals and Asset Allocation

It is important to plan a retirement savings strategy before selecting your investments. When setting financial goals, you must determine how much income you will need at retirement, and what amount of income will come from personal savings. This information will determine the size of the nest egg you need to accumulate. Once you know this amount, the next step is to develop a plan for accumulating those assets.

The theory of asset allocation is discussed in this chapter. Asset allocation helps investors achieve a fair rate of return on their investment while reducing risk through broad diversification. If practiced effectively, asset allocation helps eliminate much of the performance gap caused by market timing errors.

Chapter 15—Tax Efficient Investing

Uncle Sam wants you to pay income taxes, but you do not have to pay him right away. In fact, you can legally delay most income taxes on investment gain indefinitely, even after death. The longer you delay paying income taxes, the more money you will accumulate. A good investment plan always puts heavy emphasis on tax efficient investing. Chapter 15 links successful tax strategies with wealth accumulation.

Inflation is also a form of taxation brought about by poor fiscal and monetary policy. Since we are not in a position to change the inflation rate, we must build portfolios that adjust our retirement income for anticipated inflation.

Chapter 16—Putting it All Together

This chapter summarizes the concepts in this book by presenting a case study. A middle-aged couple has been very successful in their chosen occupations, but not so successful in investing the proceeds of their labor. This case focuses on common misconceptions discussed in this book and offers several changes to help the couple close their performance gap. Although you may see similarities with your own situation, this is only an example and is not intended to be a model for the masses. Each case is unique.

Summary

Investing for retirement can be simple, profitable, and tax efficient. By ignoring Wall Street hype and investing in a sound portfolio using market-matching strategies, you have a greater likelihood of achieving long-term success. It is the markets that make us wealthy, not complex strategies designed to beat them.

Chapter 12

Investing in the Stock Market

Most investors, both institutional and individual, will find the best way to own common stocks is through an index fund that charges minimal fees.[67]

Warren Buffett

The Indexing Alternative

The stock market, not complex strategies designed to beat the market, makes people wealthy. Why waste time and money trying to find a method that achieves superior returns when the market itself does the job perfectly well? Investors who accept the return of the stock market are likely to achieve their financial goals sooner and safer than those who follow beat-the-market strategies.

Mutual funds are the most practical way for investors to participate in the stock market. There are two types of funds, *active* and *passive*. An active fund manager attempts to select securities based on her belief that the portfolio will deliver *superior* returns. One example of an active fund is the Fidelity Magellan Fund. Its goal is to beat the S&P 500. A passive fund manager tries to match the performance of a market by purchasing all

---

67.Warren Buffett, Berkshire Hathaway 1996 Annual Report, pg 16

stocks in the same weightings as the market. Over-whelmingly, passive funds perform better than active funds. An example of a passive fund is the Vanguard Index 500 fund. It is designed to match the performance of the S&P 500.

The Performance of Active and Passive Funds

It's surprising, the number of investment advisors who think they can beat the market. But what's even more amazing is the number of clients who believe them.
—Rick Ferri

The evidence is conclusive and overwhelming. Passive stock funds achieve higher returns than most active funds. One reason for this is the inherent cost of actively managed mutual funds. Most active funds charge management fees five to six times higher than passive funds do. In addition, active managers buy and sell securities much more often than index fund managers do, increasing trading costs. Investors who choose higher-cost active funds because they are led to believe the fund will beat the market in the future are usually disappointed.

Return of General US Equity Funds
Ten Years Ending December 31, 1997

	Cumulative Rate	Annual Rate
Wilshire 5000 Equity Index*	392.4%	17.3%
Vanguard 500 Index Fund	399.1%	17.8%
Average General Equity Fund	323.1%	15.5%

*Wilshire 5000 less .30% to reflect an index fund
Source: Lipper Analytical Services

The lower return of active funds could be justified if the risk of ownership was lower or if there was a tax advantage, but neither is the case. The risk of owning active funds as measured by monthly volatility is about the same as the Wilshire 5000 index. Active funds are not "safer" than index funds. On an after-tax basis, the returns of most active funds are far lower than for index funds. The average general equity fund distributes about five times the taxable income as a comparable index fund. From all aspects—costs, taxes, and performance—stock index funds are the best way to capture the return of the stock market.

Who Uses Index Funds?

Large public pension plans and insurance companies have been using stock index funds for many years. The first index account was opened in 1974 by the Samsonite Corporation and managed by Wells Fargo Bank. The account attempted to invest in all the stocks on the New York Stock Exchange equally. The account was difficult to manage, and the style was eventually changed to indexing the S&P 500. Over the next few years, indexing become a main theme at Wells Fargo, and several large corporations started to convert their actively managed accounts to the less costly indexing alternative.

Index funds were not available to individual investors until 1976, when John Bogle of the Vanguard Group introduced the first public S&P 500 index fund for all investors. At first the popular press bashed Vanguard for starting an index fund, and other fund companies laughed at the idea. Fidelity's Chairman, Ed Johnson, scoffed at the concept. Johnson said the name of the game is to be the best, and the great mass of investors would not be satisfied with *just market returns.*

Marketing was difficult for the fledging Vanguard 500 Index Fund. It had low-management fees and a very small advertising budget. In addition, Vanguard did not pay a commission to brokers, so it was not sold through full service brokerage firms. A majority of individual investors rely on the advice of stockbrokers and other financial advisors. Advisors do not pitch index funds because they generally do not pay commissions or other fees. As a result, a typical sales presentation ends with a pitch to buy higher cost active funds that have little chance of a matching the return of market.

Investors in the Vanguard 500 Fund learned by word of mouth, and that word spread quickly in the 1990s. By 1999, the fund was vying for the top spot as the largest mutual fund in the country, second only to the Fidelity Magellan Fund. Now several companies offer index funds, including Fidelity. Still, less that 10% of the money in the stock index fund belongs to individual investors. Over 90% of index fund money belongs to institutional investors.

Structuring a Portfolio of Index Funds

A few years ago only a handful of index funds existed, and it was impossible for individual investors to develop a complete index fund portfolio. Times have changed. The number of index funds has grown by popular demand. As of this writing, over 265 index funds cover a wide variety of markets, including small-cap stocks and international markets. The wide availability of index funds has made most active management obsolete. Investors can now build portfolios of index funds that cater to their individual need without the hassle of trying to pick the next superstar fund. A portfolio of index funds is low cost and it eliminates the need to chase the hot dot. Thus, an indexing strategy helps shrink the performance gap between market returns and investor returns.

The US Stock Portion

The structure of the US stock market can be broken down by market capitalization. The largest and most successful companies in each industry make up the S&P 500 index, i.e. General Electric, Coca Cola, Microsoft. These companies have market values ranging from roughly seven billion dollars to several hundred million. The S&P 500 companies made up over 70% of the entire stock market in 1998. Few active funds have performed better than the S&P 500 over the long term.

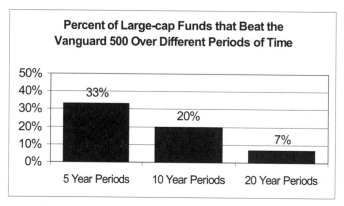

Source: Morningstar Pricipia

The remaining 30% of the US stock market is made up of mid-cap and small-cap stocks. Companies with values between $1 billion and $5 billion are considered *mid-cap* stocks and account for roughly 20% of the market. The remaining seven thousand or so *small-cap* stocks make up the final 10% of the market. Investors can purchase each segment of the market through a specific index fund, or they can purchase the entire market in the correct proportion through a total stock market index fund. If you were to purchase just a US stock fund, I strongly recommend a *total stock market index fund.*

A total stock market index fund mirrors the performance of the Wilshire 5000 Index, which is a complete composite of all actively traded US stocks. About 70% of the Wilshire 5000 is made up of large stocks; the remainder is in small to mid-size stocks.

There are several advantages to purchasing a total stock market fund. For one thing, the management fee is minimal in this type of a fund, usually 0.25% or less, compared with 1.4% for an active fund. Second, the turnover of stocks in a total market fund is exceptionally low because only a few stocks per year go in and out of the index. Third, a total stock market index fund reduces the desire for investors to chase the hot dot, since they already own all the dots. The low turnover of stocks in the fund is also good for taxable accounts because it delays capital gains.

There are several total stock market funds on the market. The oldest is the Vanguard Total Stock Market Index Fund. Competitors include the T. Rowe Price Total Stock Market Fund and the Fidelity Total Stock Market Fund. Other mutual fund companies will be introducing total stock market funds in the near future.

Indexing the US market has another inherent advantage called *style diversification.* Typically, stocks are divided into two broad styles, growth and value. Growth stocks include Microsoft and American Online and value stocks include companies like John Deere and Exxon. Index funds capture all styles of stock, so there is no need to choose one style over another. This helps reduce the performance gap.

Indexing Global Equity Markets

Since we live in the US and pay our bills in US dollars, it only makes sense to have a significant portion of our stock money in US stocks. My position is that US stocks should make up about 70% of your equity portfolio. The other 30% should be invested in international stock market index funds.

The US market is one part of a growing global stock market. In fact, the US market is becoming a smaller portion of the global market every year. In the early 1970s the US stock market accounted for 60% of the value of all stocks traded around the world. By 1998 the US portion of the global market had dropped to 35%. The growth in value of international stock markets occurred even while the US stock market went up ten-fold since the 1970s. The US share of the global market will continue to shrink as major countries like China, Russia, and India privatize large government-controlled companies.

Market Capitalization as a Percentage of the World Equity Market 1978 - 1998

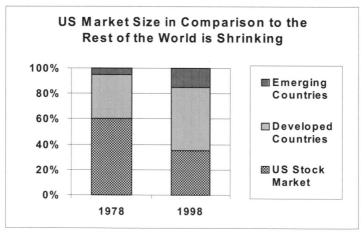

Investing in international stocks has several benefits. Over the long term, global diversification proves to be an effective tool in reducing portfolio risk, which leads to slightly higher returns. It also gives you a partial hedge against a decline in the US dollar. A portfolio with approximately a 30% position in international equities rounds out a well-diversified US stock portfolio. Some investors may prefer more or less of total holdings in international stocks. Most research on the subject recommends between 25% to 35% commitment. In either case, individuals should participate in this growth by investing a portion of their retirement money in international index funds.

Generally, the international stock market is divided into Developed Markets, which cover countries such as Japan and Germany; and Emerging Markets, which cover growing economies such as Mexico and Korea. International index funds are now available in a wide variety of those markets. You can invest in an index fund specific to each market, or invest in a total international index fund such as the Vanguard International Stock Index Fund, which covers the entire spectrum.

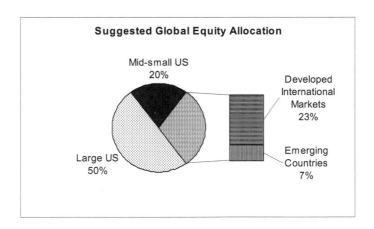

The Two-Fund Portfolio

Every veteran of the military is familiar with the acronym KISS–*keep it simple, stupid.* Indexing the portion of your portfolio devoted to stocks is a KISS strategy. By keeping it simple, you will achieve all the benefits the markets have to offer.

A portfolio of approximately 70% US index funds and 30% international index funds is an excellent lifetime portfolio for most investors, and there will be little need to change this mix over time. An investment in only two mutual funds can accomplish this goal. By placing 70% of your stock allocation in a Total Stock Market Index Fund and the remainder in a Total International Stock Index Fund, no other stock investments are needed...ever.

Von Baron once wrote, "The way to win is by not losing." Stock index funds are such a concept. By reducing the cost of investing and eliminating the desire to chase the hot dot, investors will greatly reduce the performance gap and greatly increase their retirement savings. It's that simple.

Chapter 13

Investing in the Bond Market

There are only three places to invest your money. You can buy real estate or other hard assets and hope the price moves higher. You can buy a business or a portion of one and participate in the gains of the enterprise. Or, you can let someone borrow your money and collect interest. All other investments are derivatives of these three basic types. This chapter is all about the last choice, letting people borrow your money—specifically, investing in the bond market.

Most people own bonds at some time or another during their life. If you buy a certificate of deposit at a bank, you own a bond. Investing in high-quality bonds can help stabilize an otherwise risky portfolio.

People have two options when investing in bonds. They can buy individual bonds or purchase a bond mutual fund. In many cases, buying bonds directly can lead to higher returns than investing in mutual funds. I'll explain this later. On the other hand, some categories of bonds are so complex that they should be purchased only through a fund. When purchasing a bond fund seems to be the best alternative, look for one with the lowest fee and the broadest diversification.

Bonds and Bond Mutual Funds

The US bond market is the largest in the world. Every day billions of dollars in bonds are traded at hundreds of trading desks across the country. Corporations issue bonds to finance various projects or refund maturing issues. States and cities issue tax-free municipal bonds to help build roads, hospitals, and schools. If you take a mortgage out on your home, your loan will likely become part of a mortgage pool traded in the bond market. All totaled, the US bond market is worth over $25 trillion dollars, of which five trillion are in US Treasury bonds.

You can buy individual bonds through any brokerage firm. However, I recommend a large firm because they typically carry a large inventory of bonds. In addition, large firms underwrite new issues, which is a big advantage to bond buyers. The yields on new issues are competitive and all buyers get the same rate regardless of size. If you buy five thousand dollars worth of a bond you get the same yield and pay the same price per bond as a billion dollar mutual fund. Salomon Smith Barney, Merrill Lynch, and Morgan Stanley/Dean Witter are excellent places to establish a bond account. Paine Weber is also a major underwriter of municipal bonds. A straight bond portfolio will likely perform better than a typical mutual fund with similar objectives because the investor is cutting out most costs.

Some types of bonds are complex and should only be purchased through a mutual fund. Low quality (junk) bonds, mortgages, and international bonds are a few examples. Investing in these markets is best accomplished as part of a large, diversified portfolio. While brokerage companies are a great place to buy individual bonds, they are not a good place to buy bond mutual funds. The commission cost and internal expense of broker sold products is much too high. There are a few mutual fund companies that cater to bond investors seeking low fees and expenses. The Vanguard Group offers a variety of low-cost bond funds.

Building a Simple Bond Portfolio

Building and managing a bond portfolio is a simple undertaking. Most large brokerage firms have an ample supply of high quality issues such as Treasury bonds, municipal bonds, and investment-grade corporate debt. With investment-grade bonds you don't have to worry about default risk, and the resale market for investment grade bonds is fairly liquid. In addition, you have some control over the commission you pay the broker.

You can find good books on basic bond investing available at your local library. If you decide to build a bond portfolio, it would be a good idea to read one of these books and become familiar with the terminology of bonds such as coupon, yields, par value, and other terms.

The simplest type of portfolio to manage is called a *bond ladder*. A ladder is built by purchasing bonds with maturities from one to five years (or greater). An investor then holds the bonds until maturity while collecting interest along the way. When a bond matures, you buy another five-year bond to continue the ladder.

To initially establish a ladder, take the size of your account and divide it by the number of years in the ladder. For example, using a five-year ladder and a $100,000 investment, you will buy a $20,000 bond maturing each year for the next five years. The result is the sample portfolio that follows:

Sample 5-Year Treasury Note Ladder
for a $100,000 Account

Quantity	Type of Bond	Maturity	Coupon	Price Paid	YTM
20	Treasury Note	May 2001	6.25%	102.14	5.00%
20	Treasury Note	Mar 2002	6.63%	104.02	5.12%
20	Treasury Note	Aug 2003	4.25%	96.10	5.14%
20	Treasury Note	Feb 2004	5.38%	97.17	5.24%
20	Treasury Note	Aug 2005	5.25%	99.75	5.30%

YTM = Yield to Maturity
Average Yield 5.20%

In a bond ladder, you are looking for a *yield to maturity (YTM)* or total return. For all practical purposes, the *coupon* on the bond is not a consideration. It does not matter if the bond pays 4.0% or 6.0% interest; the *price* of the bond will adjust according to current interest rates.

Once the ladder is established, you simply hold the bonds and collect interest. When a bond matures, you reinvest the $20,000 principal and $5,000 accumulated interest into another five-year bond. The result is as follows:

After the MAY 2001 Bond Matures

Quantity	Bond	Maturity	Coupon	Price Paid	YTM
20	Treasury Note	Mar 2002	6.63%	104.02	5.12%
20	Treasury Note	Aug 2003	4.25%	96.10	5.14%
20	Treasury Note	Feb 2004	5.38%	97.17	5.24%
20	Treasury Note	Aug 2005	5.25%	99.75	5.30%
25	Treasury Note	May 2006	5.31%	100.02	5.30%

Average Yield 5.22%

YTM = Yield to Maturity

Notice how the yield to maturity of the portfolio increased from 5.2% to 5.22%. This is because the maturing bond had a 5.0% YTM of the new 2006 bond has a 5.3% YTM. All things being equal, the lowest yielding year in a bond ladder is the first year. If rates remain constant over the next several years, all the new bonds will be purchased at a 5.30% yield, and eventually the yield on the portfolio will also increase to 5.3%.

A bond ladder can be five years, seven years, ten years, or longer. I do not recommend building a ladder greater than ten years for a couple of reasons. First, the longer the length of the ladder, the more the portfolio is subject to interest rate risk. If interest rates move up, a long-term bond ladder will drop in value more than a short-term portfolio. Second, many bonds are callable after ten years, and this can make managing a portfolio confusing. If a bond is callable, you do not know if it will "mature" early.

Most individually managed bond portfolios per-form better than bond mutual funds. The reason is the cost of bond funds. The average fee for a bond fund is 1.0%, which is very high considering that a typical mutual fund only makes 6.0% in interest. There is no justification for paying more than 15% of your profits out in fees. I recommend managing investment grade bond portfolios on your own.

Different Bonds for Different Purposes

The type of bonds to buy for a portfolio depends on the type of account it is. Tax-sheltered accounts such as an IRA, Profit Sharing, or Keogh should hold taxable bonds like Treasury bonds, government agency bonds, corporate bids, mortgages, certificates of deposit, and asset-backed securities. Personal accounts subject to annual income tax should consider tax-free municipal bonds. Chapter 15 discusses tax-efficient investing in greater detail.

Managing Retirement Accounts

Many retirement accounts are sheltered from current taxation. Income tax is due only when the funds are withdrawn from the account at retirement. As a result, you can buy any type of bond and not have to worry about paying taxes on the annual interest received. An efficient mix of bonds to use in a tax-sheltered portfolio is 50% government bonds and 50% corporate bonds. Using our previous example of a $100,000 portfolio and a five-year bond ladder, we could build a portfolio that looks like this hypothetical example:

Five Year Tax-Sheltered Bond Ladder
For a $100,000 Account
(Illustration only)

Quantity	Bond	Maturity	Coupon	Price Paid	YTM
10	Treasury Note	May 2001	6.25%	102.14	5.00%
10	IBM Inc.	Sep 2001	5.70%	100.20	5.50%
10	Federal Home Loan	Mar 2002	6.00%	103.02	5.35%
10	Ford Motor Credit	Jun 2002	5.80%	100.20	5.65%
10	FNMA Note	Mar 2003	4.60%	98.30	5.40%
10	Merrill Lynch Co.	Aug 2003	5.70%	100.00	5.70%
10	Fed. Farm Credit	Feb 2004	4.25%	97.10	5.50%
10	Pacific Gas & Elec.	Oct 2004	5.50%	98.00	5.75%
10	Treasury Note	Aug 2005	5.25%	99.75	5.30%
10	AT&T Inc.	Mar 2005	5.80%	100.00	5.80%

Average Yield 5.50%   YTM = Yield to Maturity

Each year an investor buys two $10,000 bonds. One bond is a government issue and the other is corporate issue. It is important to buy only recognizable, high quality corporate bonds that have an S&P rating of "A" or better. There is no sense speculating on a lower quality bond for the sake of a little more interest. By using government agency and corporate bonds, the initial yield of the portfolio jumps to 5.5%.

You could add a small amount of a high-yield (junk) bond mutual fund or similar investment to increase the yield. However, I do not recommend putting any more than 20% of the your total bond holdings into risky investments. Make sure you choose a mutual fund that is well diversified and charges a minimal fee. The Vanguard High-Yield Corporate Fund is a good example. It charges less than 0.3% per year in fees and is well diversified.

Unfortunately, you will not be able to buy Vanguard funds or any other low-cost bond fund through the same national brokerage firm where you purchase your other bonds. They do not offer access to the funds you need. You must go directly to the mutual fund company and open a second account, or purchase the fund through a mutual fund supermarket such as Schwab OneSource.

Managing Personal Accounts

Investments held in personal accounts are subject to annual income tax. In most cases, the best bonds to buy for taxable accounts are tax-free municipal bonds. Municipal bonds can put more money in your pocket than taxable bonds, especially if you are in a high tax bracket. Munis are not subject to federal or state income tax in the state where they are issued.

When comparing the yield on a muni bond to a taxable bond, you must compute the *taxable equivalent yield (TEY)*. The formula is as follows:

> **Muni Bond Yield / (1 – tax rate)**
> **For example:**
> **A muni bond yields 4% and your tax rate is 39.6%**
> **.04 / (1 - .396) = .066 or 6.6% tax equivalent yield**

A 4.0% muni bond will give you the same after-tax income as a 6.6% taxable bond if you are in the 39% tax bracket. Chances are you will not find a taxable bond of the same quality and maturity that yields 6.6% or higher.

If you live in a state that has a state income tax, it is a good idea to use municipal bonds specific to the state you pay taxes in.

There are two types of municipal bonds, general obligation (GO) and revenue. GO bonds derive revenue from tax receipts, and revenue bonds derive income from fee collection (such as a tollbooth). Some bond issuers purchase insurance from private companies to guarantee the principal on their bonds. Insured bonds generally yield less than uninsured bonds of the same issue.

Beware of AMT bonds. If you have many itemized deductions on your tax returns, do not buy bonds if the interest is subject to the Alternative Minimum Tax (AMT bonds). On the other hand, if you are not subject to AMT, the interest on AMT bonds is a little higher than other bonds of similar quality. Feel free to pick up the extra return.

Sample Five-Year Michigan Municipal Ladder For a $100,000 Account Tax Bracket = 39.5%

Qty	Bond	Rating	Maturity	Coupon	Price Paid	YTM
20	City of Troy Schools	AA	Jun 2001	4.40%	101.40	3.25%
20	State of MI GO	AA	Aug 2002	3.60%	100.00	3.60%
20	MI State Highways	AAA Insured	Oct 2003	4.00%	100.80	3.80%
20	Ann Arbor GO	A	Feb 2004	3.90%	100.00	3.90%
20	Henry Ford Hospital	A	Jul 2005	4.50%	102.50	4.00%

Average Yield 3.71%   Average Tax Equivalent Yield 6.15%
Qty = Quantity   YTM = Yield to Maturity

The tax-free yield on this portfolio is 3.71% and the tax-equivalent yield is 6.15%. Recall the yield on the taxable portfolio for retirement money was 5.50%. This gives high-income muni investors a 0.65% advantage over the taxable portfolio, or $650 per year in extra income. In the above example, Michigan has a state income tax of 4.4%, and a MI muni portfolio will save a MI resident another $100 in state income tax.

Helpful Hints for All Bond Buyers

Wall Street's primary function is to issue new stocks and bonds and create a liquid market for those securities. This includes billions of dollars in bond issues. As a result, large brokerage houses are the best place to shop for bonds, but there are some rules. When opening an account, talk to the office manager. Ask him or her to recommend a broker that does a significant portion of their business in the bond market. If you are building a municipal bond portfolio, ask for an experienced muni bond salesperson. Individual brokers that specialize in bonds have access to more inventory and are in constant contact with the bond traders.

To ensure you are getting a fair yield on a bond, check a few sources for current interest rates. The *Wall Street Journal* is a good place to begin. It includes comprehensive bond listings where you can gauge the market. Bonds trade in relation to Treasury yields, so you will want to know what the T-bond yields are. If you are buying a muni bond and have access to the Internet, check www.bloomberg.com for current yields. They have a web page devoted to the muni market, and the data is free.

The advantage of buying through a large brokerage house is the access to new issues. I recommend buying new issues whenever possible. The yield on new offerings is always competitive, and every investor gets the same rate regardless of size. You do not have to worry about the broker juicing up the commission on a new issue trade. You can also use rates on new issues to help price older bonds for sale. If a broker offers you a bond that was issued a few years ago, check the yield against new issues of similar quality.

Learn to negotiate commissions. Unless you are offered a new issue, the broker has some flexibility in the size of the commission you pay. You should always ask for the commission fee on a trade. Anything over $50 per $10,000 invested is high. Most people have no idea what commission they are paying on a bond since the fee is typically built into the price (see Chapter 4).

If you have an account at a large firm such as Salomon Smith Barney (SSB), it does not mean you are obligated to buy bonds only from that firm. You can buy bonds from other firms and have them automatically delivered into your SSB account. This type of trade is called *delivery verse payment (DVP)*. You simply open a DVP account at second firm, buy the bonds you want, and have them delivered into your account at SSB. The money is then transferred from SSB to the other firm to pay for the bonds. Using the DVP system, you can literally have a large bond account at Smith Barney and never buy a bond from them. DVP is very convenient for money managers and those who shop the street for the best deals.

The Index Fund Alternative

If you are not interested in buying individual bonds, the best alternative is to buy bond index funds. They offer immediate diversification into a wide variety of securities at a very low fee. One place to shop for low-cost bond funds is Vanguard. They have a wide variety of low cost taxable and tax-free funds to choose from.

One of the best bond index funds to use for retirement accounts is the Vanguard Intermediate-Term Bond Index fund. The fund is made up of corporate debt, government agency bonds, and treasury bonds. The portfolio has an average maturity of about seven years. If you prefer bonds with a shorter maturity, opt for the Vanguard Short-term Bond Index fund. The average maturity is only 2.7 years, about the same as a five-year bond ladder described earlier.

For municipal bond investors, Vanguard offers the Intermediate-Term Tax-Exempt Fund with an average maturity of seven years and a Limited-Term Tax-Exempt Fund with an average maturity of three years. Neither fund is an index fund, but the fees are just as low. The funds are not "state specific," meaning the bonds are from several states. As a result, your state may charge income tax on the interest.

By this time you may be wondering if I secretly work for Vanguard. The answer is no. Due largely to John Bogle's vision, Vanguard is simply the premiere supplier of index funds for individual investors. They offer the largest selection at low cost. The Vanguard Group is a not-for-profit company. By charter, the shareholders in the funds are the owners. That makes their cost structure hard to beat. According to Lipper, Inc., the average expense ratio for all Vanguard funds was 0.28% in 1998, far below the 1.25% average for the rest of the industry.

Chapter 14

Financial Goals and Asset Allocation

If you don't know where you're going, you'll end up somewhere else.

—Yogi Berra

One critical decision investors must make is to decide how much money to place in stocks and how much to place in bonds. This decision would be simple if we knew the future. If you know stocks will go up, place 100% of your money in stocks. If you know stocks will go down, a 100% bond portfolio is the only alternative. Unfortunately, life is not so simple. As we learned in Chapter 5, errors in market timing are partially responsible for part of the performance gap. Most people will find a safer solution by placing a portion of their money in stocks and a portion in bonds. This is called *strategic asset allocation decision.*

How do you determine the correct asset allocation for your account, *without trying to time the markets?* There is a right way and a wrong way to determine an appropriate allocation. The wrong way is what I call the Cosmopolitan magazine method. It is based on a questionnaire that is supposed to determine your investment psyche in ten questions or less. Many stockbrokers and other advisors try to sell commissioned investment products using the overly simplistic "Cosmo" approach. The second method of *asset allocation* is more scien-

tific. Large pension plans and other institutional investors use a liability-based approach. This method
calculates an asset allocation strategy based on the highest probability of meeting an investment goal, and
ensures that the allocation is not too risky for the client.

The Cosmo Method

Every issue of *Cosmopolitan* magazine prints a questionnaire to determine what type of person you are. For
example, "Are You a Workaholic? Answer these ten
questions and find out!" You take the quiz only to find
out you have no life or real purpose for living. The
investment industry has adopted a similar questionnaire
to determine a fast, but terribly unreliable *investment
strategy* for clients. Generally, a person is asked a series
of simple questions, and the answers are plugged into
"highly sophisticated computer model." This canned
computer program then spits out an allocation between
stocks and bonds that is supposed to represent your true
needs.

Unfortunately, the Cosmo method of asset allocation is terribly inaccurate. It oversimplifies the process
and generates riskier portfolios than would otherwise be
recommended. From a salesperson's perspective,
Cosmo models are great. They get people to invest more
in stocks and other risky assets that pay higher commissions and fees. While there is no problem in having
risky assets in a portfolio, the canned models hide the
short-term volatility that often occurs. This hidden risk
becomes a big problem for investors when markets
become volatile. A risky portfolio may sound appealing
in a bull market, but history shows that most investors
will not hold onto risky assets during a prolonged bear
market. Portfolios thrown together using a simple ten-
question quiz will lead to inadvertent market timing

mistakes in the future, which widens the performance gap.

William Sharpe, STANCO 25 Professor of Finance at Stanford University and a Nobel Prize-winning economist, calls the mass-market approach to asset allocation "Financial Planning in Fantasyland."[68] There are so many problems with the popular Cosmo model that it was not possible to include them all in this chapter. As a result, I wrote Appendix III on the subject.

Back to Basics

Why do we invest in stocks and bonds? There is no point to do so if we do not have investment goals. Though most people will say they have goals, they cannot define them. "Make a lot of money" is not a goal. "Do well" is not a goal. "Make one million dollars" is a goal. When retirement day comes, our goal is to have enough saved so that the income from our nest egg will supplement social security and private pensions to enable us to live in comfort. Investors need to know how much money they need to save and how they will reach their goal.

Prior to joining the financial services industry, I spent eight years flying fighter aircraft in the Marine Corps. Every mission I flew began with a thorough preflight plan. Although no mission flew exactly as planned, no mission flew without a plan. Investing is the same. Investment planning instills confidence, which leads to greater wealth. According to a recent survey, if two people have the same income, but one has accumulated significantly more wealth than the other, the

---

68. William F. Sharpe, "Financial Planning in Fantasyland." This paper is and expanded version of a dinner speech presented at a conference sponsored by the University of California, Davis Graduate School of Management on October 17, 1997.

wealthier person probably spent twice as much time planning his investments as the less wealthy person.[69]

For less than $50 you can buy top-of-the-line financial planning software to assist you in creating a plan. These off-the-shelf programs offer step by step instructions. The financial plan will help you understand where you are, where you would like to go, and how to get there. The process will lead you to a greater understanding of your personal mission that you need to fulfill.

Calculating a Minimum Rate of Return

One of the benefits of working a financial plan is that it isolates the *minimum required return* needed on your investments to achieve your goals. This figure is easy to calculate and will help you decide the proper mix of stocks and bonds in your portfolio. Sometimes a financial plan needs to be revised if the minimum required return is not feasible, or if the asset mix is too risky for the investor. The minimum rate of return is a mathematically derived number based on four factors:

1. The amount of money you have already saved

2. The amount you expect to save annually in the future

3. The number of years you have until retirement

4. The minimum amount needed at retirement

Once you have the information above, a minimum return can be derived using a simple annuity calculation

---

69. Thomas J. Stanley, Ph.D. and William D. Danko, Ph.D., The Millionaire Next Door, Pocket Books, New York, NY, 1996, pg 97

found on any financial calculator, spreadsheet, or financial planning program. Most people can come up with the first three points, but they have trouble with the fourth one—understanding when they have enough to retire. This is not difficult to figure out as long as your lifestyle is not going to change radically in retirement. To find the amount you need at retirement, following these simple steps:

1. Take your average annual income before tax and subtract the amount you save each year. That is the amount you spend.

2. Multiply your spending amount by 20 to come to your initial minimum retirement amount.

3. Adjust the amount for inflation.

Here is an example of the process:

1. A 50-year-old man earns $100,000 per year and has $700,000 in savings. He spends $85,000 per year (including taxes) and saves $15,000. He would like to retire at age 65 and live the same lifestyle.

2. Multiply $85,000 times 20 to find the initial minimum retirement amount of $1,700,000. Adjust for a 2.0% annual inflation rate over the next 15 years and the *inflation adjusted* minimum amount needed at retirement is $2,300,000.

3. Using a financial calculator, plug in a $700,000 present value, a $2,300,00 ending value, deposits of $15,000 per year, and run for 15 years. The result is an implied rate of return of 7.0%.

4. If the man's account compounds at 7.0% over the next 15 years, he will reach his goal at retire-

ment. He can then withdraw 5.0% of the account each year for the rest of his life. Any extra earnings will stay in the account as an inflation hedge.

In the example above, we have left out a few things. We assumed the man has only income from savings and no other at retirement. In reality, he will probably receive Social Security and possibly a pension. He may also receive an inheritance or sell real estate. These adjustments could be factored into the model as well.

Calculating Maximum Risk Tolerance

In our example above, we calculated the minimum required return of 7.0%. What asset allocation between stocks and bonds has a high probability of reaching this goal? Recall from Chapter 11 the following data:

Future Estimates of Stocks, Bonds, and Inflation

Benchmark	Estimate 2000-2030
Inflation Rate	2%
Bond Returns (nominal)	5%
Bonds – Inflation adjusted	3%
Stock Returns (nominal)	8%
Stocks – Inflation adjusted	6%

Using the information in the table, a 7.0% return implies about a 65% position in the stock market earning 8.0% and a 35% position in the bond market earning 5.0%. Mathematically this works out to 7.0%. Theoretically, a 65/35 split would be the correct allocation, but is that a reasonable portfolio for a 50-year-old man with fifteen years to retirement? Can the man handle the risk implied in 65% stock position? Does the level of risk implied by the required 7.0% return match his personality? It depends on the man's tolerance for risk.

If a person invests heavily in stocks because it is what he thinks he needs to make his retirement account work, he may be doing himself more harm than good. If an asset allocation is beyond the envelope of a person's risk tolerance, there is a strong potential he will sell out of stocks during a bear market. That destroys the entire plan and significantly reduces return.

Stress Testing an Asset Allocation

Frequently I meet people who say another advisor recommended a more aggressive asset allocation than I have. Normally, the other advisor has used the typical Cosmo questions and came up with a greater allocation toward stocks, which of course pays that advisor higher commissions and fees. To show the client there is more to an asset allocation than a simple questionnaire, I use the *73-74 Stress Test*.

Imagine holding a majority of your portfolio in stocks during the 1973-74 bear market when the averages fell over 40% and inflation was raging. Would you have stayed in? Most investors didn't. Using the 1973-74 time period to stress test a portfolio is a great tool. Every financial advisor should learn to use it so they can understand their clients' true reaction to a bear market.

In this example we will use a portfolio of 65% stocks and 35% bonds. Historically that allocation has a good chance of producing a 7.0% required return over a 15-year period. Let us assume it is the beginning of 1973, and our "client" agrees to our 65/35 allocation. Using the data from our example above, our client invests $700,000 and will add $15,000 per year going forward. Here is the initial allocation:

Initial Portfolio Allocation
January 1973

Stocks (65%) S&P 500	Bond (35%) 5 yr. Treasury	Total Account
$450,000	$250,000	$700,000

It was a terrible year in 1973. The stock market fell almost 15%, and the economy was on shaky ground. Our client lost over $50,000. It was time to balance the portfolio and add another $15,000 for this year's contribution to the plan.

Portfolio Value
December 1973

Stocks S&P 500	Bond 5 yr. Treasury	Total Account
$384,000	$262,000	$646,000
	Plus new cash	+15,000
	Total at year end	$661,000

The asset allocation of the portfolio is out of kilter. In order to go back to a 65% stock 35% bond position, our client needs to buy $46,000 worth of stocks and sell $31,000 worth of bonds. He is reluctant, but decides to go along with the plan.

New Portfolio Allocation
January 1974

Stocks (65%) S&P 500	Bond (35%) 5 yr. Treasury	Total Account
$430,000	$231,000	$661,000

As it turned out, 1974 was worse than 1973. The stock market fell over 26%, and the economy was flat on its back. Not to mention the President resigned, and the Arab oil embargo was in full swing. Our client lost over $100,000 in 1974. It was time to balance the portfolio and add another $15,000 for this year's contribution.

Portfolio Value
December 1974

Stocks S&P 500	Bond 5 yr. Treasury	Total Account
$316,000	$244,000	$560,000
	Plus new cash	+15,000
	Total at year end	$575,000

The portfolio needs to be balanced again. In order to put it back to a 65% stock 35% bond position, our client needs to buy $59,000 worth of stocks and sell $44,000 worth of bonds. So far he has lost $155,000 since he started with our strategy, and he is two years closer to retirement.

Proposed New Portfolio Allocation
January 1975

Stocks (65%) S&P 500	Bond (35%) 5 yr. Treasury	Total Account
$375,000	$200,000	$575,000

You plan to call the client to relay this information, but you do not need to because he will likely call you! He no longer wants to have so much in stocks, they are too risky and he is losing too much money. He wants you to put most of the money in the Treasury bond portfolio. He will consider leaving $100,000 or so in the market when it goes up. So much for the Cosmo approach to asset allocation.

A More Conservative Approach

Let's go back to the beginning of 1973. Instead of choosing a portfolio of 65% stocks and 35% bonds we recommend the opposite, a portfolio of 35% stock and 65% bonds. Our client agreed to our allocation and we invest his $700,000 as follows:

Initial Portfolio Allocation
January 1973

Stocks (35%) S&P 500	Bond (65%) 5 yr. Treasury	Total Account
$245,000	$455,000	$700,000

In 1973 the stock market fell almost 15%, and the economy was poor. Our client lost a little. It was time to call the client to discuss his options and add another $15,000 for this year's contribution.

Portfolio Value
December 1973

Stocks S&P 500	Bond 5 yr. Treasury	Total Account
$209,000	$470,000	$679,000
	Plus new cash	+15,000
	Total at year end	$694,000

In order to put it back to a 35% stock 65% bond position, our client needs to buy $34,000 worth of stocks and sell $19,000 worth of bonds. We call the client, and he agrees to this.

New Portfolio Allocation
January 1974

Stocks S&P 500	Bond 5 yr. Treasury	Total Account
$243,000	$451,000	$694,000

The following year, 1974 was worse than 1973 and the stock market fell over 26%.

Portfolio Value
December 1974

Stocks S&P 500	Bond 5 yr. Treasury	Total Account
$178,000	$477,000	$655,000
	Plus new cash	+15,000
	Total at year end	$670,000

Proposed New Portfolio Allocation
January 1975

Stocks S&P 500	Bond 5 yr. Treasury	Total Account
$235,000	$435,000	$670,000

We call the client for his $15,000 contribution and explain that it is time to balance the portfolio back to 35% stock, 65% bond position. The client is reluctant, but eventually decides to stick with the plan. He gives us permission to re-balance the portfolio. *The 35% stock, 65% bond allocation worked for this client because it is was not beyond his risk tolerance.* It passes the *73-74 Stress Test.*

The portfolio with an initial 65% in stocks was too risky for the client, and he used *market timing* to reduce his allocation to stocks at *precisely the wrong time.* A better allocation would have been 35% of his portfolio in stocks because the client stayed with the portfolio during the entire period, even during the worst market conditions. In 1975, stocks were up 37% and in 1976 the market gained another 24%. As a result, *the conservative portfolio made more money than the aggressive one!*

Moral of the Story

Risk comes from not knowing what you are doing.[70]
—Warren Buffett

A large position in stocks may sound appealing after a strong bull market, but most people find it difficult to stick with a high allocation during a bear market. It is important to understand the risks in the market and

---

70. James Rassmussen, "Buffett Talks Strategy with Students," *Omaha World-Herald,* Jan 2, 1994, pg 17s

how you will handle them. Asset allocations work over long periods of time *only* if investors keep the same allocation during the entire period. The asset allocation you should choose is one you can stick with during all market conditions over a very long time. The highest yielding portfolio is not the one with the most stocks. It is the one that is within the risk tolerance of the investor. A lower allocation to stocks will yield a higher long-term return if investors respond appropriately in a bear market.

Chapter 15

Tax-Efficient Investing

*For all long-term investors, there is only one objective –
maximum total real return after taxes.*

—Sir John Templeton[71]

Uncle Sam wants you...to pay income taxes. But you
don't have to pay him right away. In fact, you can
legally delay most income taxes on investment gains
indefinitely, even after death. The longer you delay paying income tax, the more money you have working for
you and the more you will accumulate. A good investment plan always puts heavy emphasis on tax-efficient
investing.

How Taxes Affect
Market Returns

If you ask a friend how much money she made last year,
she will likely quote a figure based on her annual salary.
This figure may be a fair indication of her gross income,
but it is not an indication of how much money she made.
Our silent partners, the Federal and State Governments,

---

71. Excerpts from *The Templeton Touch* by William Proctor,
quoted in Classics, ed. Charles D. Ellis (Homewood, Ill.: Dow
Jones-Erwin, 1989), p. 738

take a large cut (sometimes local governments as well). Net income is what is left after paying income tax.

Investment gains are also subject to income tax. Tax is due each year if the income or gain is realized in personal account, and it is due when funds are withdrawn from a tax-sheltered retirement account. Either way, Uncle Sam will get paid eventually.

In a personal account, your tax rate on investment gain depends on the nature of the income. Interest, dividends, and short-term capital gains are subject to ordinary income tax at your regular tax rate. If you have realized a gain on assets held for more than one year, a lower capital gains tax is applied. On a year-after-year basis, the payment of taxes on investment returns can significantly lower your investment performance.

U.S. Financial Markets Before and After Tax Returns 1926-1994

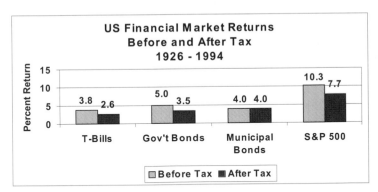

Source: Siegal & Montgomery, *Journal of Portfolio Management,* Winter 1995

One of the few taxes not reflected in the chart above is the *inflation* tax. Poor government monetary and fiscal policy creates inflation, which erodes the purchasing power of dollars earned and cripples the real value of our retirement savings. Although government policy creates inflation, Congress does not allow us to recognize it when figuring our taxable income. As a result, we pay tax on investment gain as though no inflation existed. Since 1926, the inflation rate has averaged about 3.0%, and the after tax return on Treasury bills has been about 2.6%. Therefore, after adjusting for inflation, all the gains from T-bills were lost and then some.

Taxes and Mutual Fund Returns

There are those who make money in the market, and those who keep it.

—Bengaman Graham

Taxes can have a devastating effect on mutual fund returns. In Part I of this book we measured the performance gap of mutual fund investors on a pre-tax basis. If we were to measure the gap on an after-tax basis, it would be much larger. Over a 20-year period, less that 10% of surviving large-cap mutual funds have performed better than the S&P 500 on a pre-tax basis. On an after-tax basis, the number drops much lower. Perhaps only one or two funds beat the market. John Bogle, Chairman of the Vanguard Group, in a speech during the summer of 1997 stated the problem clearly:

> Portfolio managers, fund sponsors, and distributors know that funds don't pay much, if any, attention to tax concerns. This important fact should be stated in the prospectus: "This fund is managed without regard to tax considerations, and, given its expected rate of portfolio turnover, is likely to realize and distribute a high portion of its capital return in the form of capital gains which are taxable annually, a substantial portion of which is likely to be realized in the form of short-term gains subject to full income tax rates."

In a 1998 presentation for the Association for Investment Management and Research (AIMR), Bogle compared the returns of actively managed stock funds to index funds on a pre-tax and an after tax basis. Bogle used an average turnover rate of 80% for active funds in his example. This was the average turnover for all US equity funds in 1997 as reported by Morningstar. His example assumes a market return of 10%:

Index Funds After-tax Versus Active Funds After-tax

	Gross Return	Expenses	Pre-tax	Taxes	After Fees & Tax
Average Actively Mgd Fund	10%	2.0%	8.0%	1.5%	6.5%
Buy and Hold Index Fund	10%	0.2%	9.8%	0.8%	9.0%

Bogle's example clearly shows one hidden advantage of index funds. Fees and taxes reduce the return of the average actively managed fund by 3.5%. A full 35% of the total gain is lost to fees and expenses. On the other hand, the index fund returned 9.0% after fees and taxes. Only 10% of the total gain was lost due to fees and taxes.

The problem of mutual fund taxation can be shocking to investors. In 1997 some people got caught in the volatile overseas markets. Mutual funds with a high concentration of stocks in Asian economies lost significant value. But that wasn't the end of the story. Many investors who lost money were also hit with significant capital gains distributions at the end of the year. This means they had to pay taxes even though they *lost money* on their investment. For example, Investco Asian Growth Fund distributed 21% of its net asset value during December 1997 after losing 38.5% during that year. An investor who put $10,000 in the fund at the beginning of the year would have lost $3,850 by December 31 and paid taxes on a $1,300 capital gain distribution! Talk about adding insult to injury.

Tax Strategies You Can Use

Several strategies can help you limit your taxable income on investment gains. Here is a partial list:

1. Use tax-sheltered retirement accounts such as an IRA and 401(k)

2. Use tax-friendly investments in personal accounts

3. Dollar cost average index funds in personal accounts to establish different tax-lots

4. Stay away from high cost tax shelters such as variable annuities and other packaged products

5. Spend taxable money first in retirement

Tax-Sheltered Accounts

The Government wants the public to save for retirement, so Congress has established a number of qualified accounts doing so. If you put money into these accounts each year, you can deduct the amount from taxable income. Investors should participate to the fullest extent in all the tax-sheltered accounts set up by Congress. These include IRA, 401(k), Roth IRA, and similar qualified savings vehicles. They do *not* include high cost variable annuities and other insurance products. If you own a business or are self-employed, consider opening a prototype pension offered through a low-cost provider such as Vanguard, Schwab, or other no-load mutual fund company.

Use Tax-friendly Investments in Personal Accounts

Chapter 13 on fixed income investing discussed the advantages of tax-free municipal bonds in a personal account. For most people, munis make the most money on an after-tax basis.

For the stock portion of your taxable portfolio, the low turnover of a stock index fund is a huge benefit. The dividend and capital gain distribution of the average index fund is about one-fifth that of the average actively managed stock fund. This means less tax to pay each year. Over the past five years, Vanguard has introduced a number of *tax-managed index funds*. These popular portfolios are even more tax-efficient than a standard S&P 500 index fund. They use a variety of tax-efficient management techniques to ensure that taxable gains, dividend and interest distributions are held to a minimum.

Dollar Cost Average into Index Funds and Use Tax-swaps

For your personal account I recommend buying stock index funds over a period of time rather that jumping in the market all at once. This concept has nothing to do with the direction of the market or with a market timing strategy. Instead, it has to do with establishing different tax lots for your mutual fund shares. It is likely that sometime during the year the stock market will trade at a lower value than the price of some of your tax lots.

You can use this as an opportunity to tax swap from one index fund to another and establish a permanent tax loss without ever leaving the market.

The IRS does not allow you to do a *tax wash* with individual stocks. In other words, you cannot sell a stock at a loss, take the tax deduction, and immediately buy the same stock back. You must wait thirty days to buy it back. However, in an index fund tax swaps are different. Since there are many index funds offered by various companies, you can swap out of one company's index fund and into another, and it is *not* considered to be a tax wash. For example, it is acceptable if you sell a tax lot in the Vanguard Total Stock Market Index Fund and immediately buy the Fidelity Total Market Fund. Since the funds are offered by two different mutual fund companies, they are not considered "virtually identical" securities, and a tax swap (not a tax wash) is perfectly legal. Under this scenario you can take a tax loss while remaining fully invested in the market.

Tax swaps on municipal bonds are similar. You can sell one bond at a loss and buy anther with (close to) the same yield and maturity. Be careful with muni swaps, however; the rules are more complex.

I recommend consulting your tax accountant before proceeding with any tax swap.

Stay away from high-cost tax shelters such as limited partnerships, variable annuities, and other packaged products

If you like permanent frustration and want to go years without seeing your money, if ever, buy a tax-sheltered limited partnership. Many high-commission, low potential tax shelters should be bought only by the very knowledgeable. Unfortunately, they often end up being sold to the naive. I have heard of only a few tax-shelter partnerships that actually worked the way they were supposed to. Congress loves to close loopholes on tax shelters just about the time the public embraces the idea. I highly recommend staying away from limited partnerships with your retirement money.

I also advise against buying a variable annuity if you can avoid doing so. The insurance aspect of the variable annuity is not worth the price you pay. In fact, it is the *most expensive life insurance you will ever own.* Hundreds of thousands of stockbrokers, insurance salespeople, and independent advisors are on the prowl selling these high-cost products strictly for the commission they earn. There are better ways to invest. A stock index fund generates greater wealth in the long term, and the income taxes and estate taxes are much lower.

If you already own a variable annuity, do a 1035 transfer to the Vanguard Variable Annuity Plan. Vanguard offers a product that has index funds within an annuity, so the fees are much lower than the typical broker-sold product. In addition, there is no commission built into the price of the insurance, so the fees are only a fraction of the cost of fees for broker-sold products.

I advise my clients to stay away from "investing" in other insurance products as well. This includes variable life, whole life, and other high-cost insurance products that are disguised as an investment. If you need life insurance, "buy term and invest the rest."

Spend Taxable Money First in Retirement

When you finally retire, your savings will likely be in two forms—tax-sheltered accounts and personal accounts. The government requires minimum distributions from tax-sheltered accounts once you turn age 70 and a half. The minimum distribution is based on your life expectancy. Ordinary income tax is due when the money is distributed.

If you retire prior to age 70 and a half, spend your personal savings first. You have already paid tax on this money and will not be taxed again. To the extent that you need to liquidate stocks or index funds to meet current obligations, you will find that the tax rate on long-term capital gains is lower than it is for ordinary income. This is why it makes sense to liquidate personal investments before taking a taxable distribution from a retirement account.

The Laws are Always Changing

The tax code is always changing. Congress tinkers with tax rates and methods of collecting tax almost every year. The investment strategies discussed in this book are flexible and can adapt quickly to changes in the code. It pays to stay abreast of tax law changes and to seek the help of a qualified tax accountant.

Chapter 16

Putting it All Together

I would rather be certain of a good return than hopeful of a great one.

—Warren Buffett

Old habits die hard. It is not easy to abandon a method of investing that you may have been using for years. The illusion of high returns is hard to turn away from. After all, we have been programmed all our lives to seek superior performance through a "beat the market" approach. A few lucky investors may beat the odds, but the other 99% fall far short. The world is full of sales people who make a living dangling the illusion of low-risk high-yield returns in front of you. Wise investors peer through the sales hype and look at the real risks and returns.

The concepts presented in this book are simple and straightforward, but may take a few years to implement. Money tends to suffer from *inertia.* People act slowly when embracing a new investment philosophy. Closing an account with a friendly broker or advisor is often difficult. It helps to remember that the broker or advisor has been *well paid* for services in the past and that it is simply time for you to move to greener pastures.

If you take time to define your investment goals, select an appropriate asset allocation strategy, plan a tax strategy, and make a long-term commitment to low-cost investing, you have the greatest chance for success.

Once you implement your new approach to investing, it takes only a few hours each year to maintain it. There is no need to waste valuable time and money trying to find strategies that beat the street. Your rewards for following this approach include greater wealth, lower cost, lower risk, lower frustration levels, and lower taxes.

Case Study

It requires a great deal of boldness and a great deal of caution to make a great fortune; and when you have it, it requires ten times the as much wit to keep it.
—Meyer Rothschild

This chapter sums up important concepts by presenting them in a case study. A middle-aged couple has been successful in their chosen occupation, but not very successful investing the fruits of their labors. After a review of their current strategy, the investment counselor suggests several changes to get them on the right track. Although you may see similarities with your own situation, this is only an example and is not intended to be a model for the masses.

Bob and Betty Barnet are married and have two children ages 19 and 21, both in college. They have enough income to cover their children's education, and are now focusing on saving for retirement. The Barnets would like to retire in twenty years when they both reach age 65. They own a medium-sized business that generates about $150,000 per year before income tax.

Bob and Betty have recently established a pension and a profit-sharing plan for their business at a local bank. It is invested in the bank's proprietary mutual funds and a money market fund. So far they have accumulated $30,000 for themselves in the plan and believe they can invest $30,000 each year from now on. They also have $150,000 in personal savings, most of which is in a savings account at the bank and in a few stocks Mr. Barnet has bought through the years.

The Barnets currently spend about $8,000 per month pre-tax or $96,000 per year, although $24,000 per year is going to tuition and other college costs. When the children are done with school and on their own, the Barnets figure they will need a monthly income of $6,000 per month to cover all their needs.

Step 1. Defining the Barnets' Position and Goals

- The Barnets would like to sell their business and retire in twenty years at age 65. This means saving enough while working so that they can draw a reasonable income while in retirement. They feel $6,000 per month would be sufficient.

- The Barnets do not believe their business is worth much once they retire. Since it is a consulting business, when Bob and Betty go, the clients will likely move on. For this reason, they value the book of business at one times earnings, or roughly $100,000.

- So far the Barnets have saved $180,000 for retirement and believe they can put away $30,000 annually from here on. They also think they will be able save more once the children are out of college and out of the house.

Step 2. Adjusting the Numbers for Inflation

- The Barnets believe inflation will average about 2.0% over the remainder of their life. Adjusting $6,000 by 2.0% inflation for twenty years equals about $9,000 per month needed at retirement, or an annual inflation-adjusted income $107,000 per year.

- Assume a portion of this income will come from Social Security. Let's guess Social Security pays the Barnets a total of $2,000 per month at age 65. This figure is lower than the current rate and is not adjusted for inflation, but it is probably closer to reality than what the Social Security Administration is quoting.

- Less social security income, the Barnets need to withdraw $7,000 per month from savings to meet their $9,000 income goal. If we multiply $7,000 by 12 months, they need $84,000 per year after social security.

- To find the total savings needed at retirement, multiply $84,000 by 20. This means at age 65 the Barnets need a nest egg of approximately $1,700,000. For the purpose of this illustration, assume their business does not have any value once the Barnets retire. Also assume they do not increase their $30,000 savings rate in the future.

- By withdrawing 5.0% per year from their $1,700,000 account, the Barnets will have income of $85,000 per year adjusted for inflation, plus $24,000 from Social Security. This gives them the $9,000 per month they desire.

Step 3. Determine the Minimum Required Rate of Return

- The next step is to calculate the minimum required rate of return on the Barnets' investment portfolio. Using a spreadsheet program like Microsoft Excel, or financial planning software like Quicken, you can calculate the return they need to meet their financial goal.

- The Barnets currently have $180,000 in savings and need to accumulate a minimum of $1,700,000 over the next 20 years. They can put away $30,000 per year. Using software or a financial calculator, input $180,000 as the present value of the investment, add contributions of $30,000 per year, put in 20 years for time and an ending value of $1,700,000. Your computer or calculator should produce a required return of 6.1%.

- If the Barnets save exactly as planned and the account grows at an annual rate of 6.1% per year, they will have the $1,700,000 they need at retirement.

In this simple model we found that the Barnets have a *future liability* of $1,700,000. Using the data provided to us, we calculated a minimum required rate of return on their savings to *match* the liability. This method is close to the model used by large pension funds to calculate their required return.

If a person's money flows can be determined and an accurate assumption about inflation can be made, then a required rate of return can be easily found. Obviously, situations change, and this plan is based on everything we know about the Barnets today. In the future they could buy another business, lose their current business, retire early, win the lottery, get sick, get divorced, inherit money, etc. Life can be unpredictable, but we still need to plan.

This case study is not over. Next we need to find an asset allocation that fits the required rate of return and the Barnets' tolerance toward risk.

Market Expectations and Asset Allocation

We have calculated Barnets' required return to be a 6.1% assuming a 2.0% inflation rate. Now it is time to choose actual investments to meet their goals. We are looking for an investment portfolio that has the highest probability of achieving at least a 6.1% rate of return over twenty years with the lowest possible risk factor.

If there were a risk-free way to earn 6.1% annual return, the Barnet's should seriously consider that option. There is no reason to take more risk than is necessary to match an investment goal. We are only seeking an investment plan that will give the Barnets what they truly desire, a stable and secure retirement.

Over the long term, risk-free Treasury bonds have returned only about 3.0% over inflation. This means a portfolio of Treasury bonds will return about 5.0% over the next twenty years. A portfolio of T-bonds leaves the Barnets short of their retirement goal. They must assume some risk in order to increase the probability of reaching a 6.1% return.

Suggested Portfolio for the Barnets' Expected Return of Stocks and Bonds

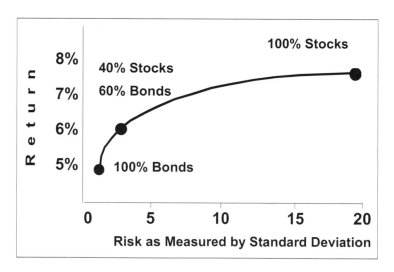

Using the expected return of the markets discussed in Chapter 11, a portfolio invested in 40% stocks and 60% bonds has a high probability of producing a 6.1% return in the future. Assuming a 2.0% inflation rate, the above chart reflects this allocation. This chart also assumes the portfolio has been balanced to a 40/60 stock/bond mix each year.

Notice that the return line, while moving from bonds to stocks, is curved. This is a "free lunch" from asset allocation. Your return (left scale) moves up as you add stocks to a 100% bond portfolio, but the risk level (bottom scale) does not move in the same proportion. Because stocks and bonds are two different asset classes, you can increase your return by adding some stocks to a portfolio, with very little increase in risk. As a result, a balanced portfolio of stocks and bonds is more efficient than a portfolio of all bonds or all stocks.

Risk Tolerance

In order for an account to grow after taxes and inflation, the portfolio must take some risk. History shows the long-term return from a risk-free T-bill portfolio is negative after taxes and inflation.[72] While some risk is necessary, if a person assumes too much risk, the tendency is to abandon a plan at the wrong moment, causing poor performance over the long term. Added risk means added volatility. There are times when a portfolio will go down in value. Investors must be prepared to see their account value go down once in a while. How a person reacts to such temporary losses is extremely important.

Every investor needs to answer two questions. First, how much risk do you *need* to take? Second, how much risk are you *capable* of taking? If an investor takes more risk than he needs or assumes more risk than he can handle, he is making a critical mistake. A portfolio should have a low enough risk level so the investor

---

72. According to Ibbotson Associates, since 1926 an investor in 100% Treasury bill would have compounded at a –0.9% return after tax and inflation.

will not be compelled to change the asset allocation during adverse market conditions.

In our example, if the Barnets hold a 40% stock, 60% bond portfolio throughout their working years, there is a good chance they will reach their financial goal at retirement. They need to be prepared to buy stocks during poor market conditions and sell stocks when the market moves higher. As a competent investment advisor we must determine to the best of our ability if the Barnets can handle the risk implied in a 40% stock, 60% bond allocation.

There is no easy way to assess risk. Most people claim they are risk takers, but history has proven otherwise. One way to gauge the risk tolerance of an investor is to work the *73-74 Stress Test* explained in Chapter 14. The test would determine if the Barnets could have held onto a 40/60 allocation during the 73-74 bear market. If they do hold their position, there is a good chance this allocation will work for them in the future.

All successful investors know their personal risk limits, though they may describe them differently. Warren Buffett invests within his *circle of competence*. Benjeman Graham only bought stocks that had a high *margin of safety*. International investor Sir John Templeton does not invest in a country until there is *blood in the streets*. These people thought long and hard about controlling risk. As Warren Buffett reminds us, "Risk comes from not knowing what you are doing."

Case Study Recommendations

Here is my recommendation for the Barnets:

- Save $30,000 per year in the sheltered retirement plan to avoid current income tax. It is always better to save with pre-tax dollars than after-tax dollars. See Chapter 15.

- Move the pension account from the bank to a low-cost fund mutual fund company. This has several advantages. First, it will save thousands of dollars in bank fees over the years; second, it gets the plan out of the bank's proprietary (high fee) mutual funds and into a company that has low-cost index funds.

- Once the pension account is reestablished at the mutual fund company, the Barnets should invest 60% in an intermediate term bond index fund, 25% in a US total stock market index fund, and 15% in a total international stock index fund. This is a great mix for long-term investors. Each year, after a new contribution is made, they should balance the portfolio back to its original weighting. See Chapter 12.

- With $100,000 in personal money, build a five-year municipal bond ladder. Place $20,000 per year in high quality bonds that mature in each of the next five years. The Barnets should use a broker at a large, established brokerage firm and ask for only new issue munis. See Chapter 13.

- Place $30,000 of personal money in a market fund at a brokerage house. This is emergency money. Money market funds at brokerage houses pay higher interest rates than the banks do. Almost every brokerage house offers checking services. It helps to have checks for quick access to your money and in case you need cash on a weekend.

- Finally, leave Bob $20,000 in personal money to play the stock market. He enjoys following the market and picking a few stocks now and then. I recommend buying stocks in a personal account because the losses can provide tax deductions. For planning purposes, the account should not be expected to grow over the years, or counted on in retirement. See Appendix II.

The recommendations in this case study focus on the four rules of a solid retirement savings plan:

1. Keep investment costs low by sticking to stock index funds and straight bonds;

2. Diversify stock holdings across a wide spectrum of index funds;

3. 4. Use a consistent asset allocation between stocks and bonds, and do not try to time the market;

4. 5. Implement a sound tax strategy.

These four rules will add more wealth to more retirement savers than anything else Wall Street has to offer. The more you think about these rules, the more they become clear. Following them will make your investment plan a success.

Concluding Remarks

Truth must be repeated again and again, because error is constantly being preached around it.
—Johann Wolfgnag Von Goethe

I hope you have enjoyed reading *Serious Money*! As each day passes, the information in this book becomes more relevant. During his 1999 State of the Union Address, President Clinton acknowledged the impending crisis in Social Security. As we become more responsible for our own retirement income, costs must come down and investment skills must improve.

Contrary to popular belief, there is no secret formula to saving for retirement. Meeting your retirement needs requires a long-term commitment. The concepts in this book promote an investment philosophy that has a high probability of success because it ignores Wall Street hype and cuts costs. A strategy based on indexing the markets will work for you because it is simple, low cost, and is not speculative. Going forward with your retirement saving plan, always remember that *the markets make people wealthy, not complex strategies designed to beat them.*

APPENDICES

Calculating Your Investment Performance

The Association for Investment Management and Research (AIMR) in Charlottesville, Virginia, develops and maintains performance presentation standards for the investment industry. The Security and Exchange Commission has final approval over the standards. The information in this appendix is derived from the AIMR Performance Presentation Standards Handbook available through AIMR.[73]

You can measure the performance of an account in many different ways; however, *time weighting* is the industry's standard. A time-weighted return (TWR) measures the performance of an account over a specific period of time. Units of time are linked together to form longer returns. For example, monthly returns are linked together to establish quarterly returns, which are linked to establish annual returns, and so forth.

Starting in the year 2000, AIMR requires performance to be calculated monthly. However, a quarterly

---

73. The Association of Investment Management and Research is located in Charlottesville, Virginia. A copy of the AIMR Performance Presentation Standard Handbook is available from AIMR at a nominal fee. Phone 804 980-3668 or visit the AIMR web site at www.aimr.com.

calculation works fine for the average investor who does not make large deposits or withdrawals. For quarters when large deposits or withdrawals are made, a person should calculate monthly. Daily calculation of returns is the most accurate, but this can be costly and requires a fairly sophisticated methodology.

It is important to understand exactly what a time-weighted return measures, so you will not be misled. A time-weighted return accurately measures the performance of an account over a specific period of time and not the amount of money gained or lost in the account. A TWR is strictly an accounting tool used to compare one account against another. It does not tell you actual dollars gained or lost. Nevertheless, it will help you keep track of your investments and your investment advisors.

The following guide will help you calculate your personal time-weighted return:

1. Assume you begin the year with $100 in an account and by the end of the first quarter (March 31) the account value is $110.

2. The basic formula is fairly straightforward. Take the ending balance minus the beginning balance divided by the beginning balance. For example, the balance was $100 on January 1 and ended at $110 on March 31. The $10 gain is divided by $100 for a return of 10%. This assumes that no contributions or withdrawals were made during the quarter.

Beginning Balance (BB)	Ending Balance (EB)	(EB – BB)/ BB	Quarterly Return
$100	$110	(110 – 100) /100	.10 = 10.0%

3. The calculation becomes more complex if money is added or subtracted from the account.

The formula now expands to (ending balance – ½ contributions + ½ withdrawals) divided by (beginning balance + ½ contribution – ½ withdrawals) minus 1. Assume your beginning balance was $100, the ending balance was $110, and you added $5 in the middle of the period.

Beginning Balance (BB)	Contribution [C] or Withdrawal (W)	Ending Balance (EB)	[(EB – ½ C + ½ W) / (BB + ½ C – ½ W)] –1	Quarterly Return
$100	$5	$110	[(110 – 2.5)/(100 + 2.5)] –1	.049 = 4.9%

4. Calculating annual return requires *linking* quarterly returns together. This is accomplished by adding a "1" to each quarterly return and multiplying them together, then subtracting "1" at the end. Assume the first quarter return was 4.9%, second quarter was 1.1%, third quarter was 1.6%, and fourth quarter was 2.0%. The return for the year is as follows:

Linking Quarterly Returns

Quarter	Percent Return	Change to Decimal	Add "1"	Multiply
First	4.9%	.049	1.049	1.049
Second	1.1%	0.011	1.011	x 1.011
Third	-1.6%	-.016	.994	x 0.994
Fourth	2.0%	.020	1.020	x 1.020
		Multiply four quarters and subtract 1		

Multiply and subtract "1" = (1.049 x 1.011 x 0.994 x 1.020) – 1 = .075 or 7.5%.

5. The annual return for the example is 7.5%. This figure should be compared to an appropriate index to determine if the account was performing up to expectations. If the account was invested in large US stocks, an appropriate benchmark may be the S&P 500. A complete list

of index returns can be found in *Barron's* at the end of each quarter. *Barron's* also lists Lipper Mutual Fund returns to help you compare the performance of your fund to the average mutual fund in its category.

6. The following table should help you calculate your return:

Finding Annual Returns Using Quarterly Data

Beginning Quarterly Balance (BB)	Contributions or Withdrawals (CW)	Ending Quarterly Balance (EB)	Quarterly Return (EB - 1/2 CW) - BB/ (BB + 1/2 CW)	Quarterly Return + 1	Multi Quarters
1st Quarter					
2nd Quarter					
3rd Quarter					
4th Quarter					
				Multiply four quarters and subtract 1	

7. In some quarters, a large contribution or withdrawal can distort returns. During periods of large cash flows, it is better to link returns monthly to find an accurate quarterly return. To do this, calculate the return each month of the quarter, then link the three monthly returns together.

Finding Quarterly Returns Using Monthly Data

Beginning Monthly Balance (BB)	Contributions or Withdrawals (C or W)	Ending Monthly Balance (EB)	Monthly Returns (EB − ½ C + ½ W) / (BB + ½ C − ½ W)] −1	Monthly Return + 1	Multi Mnth
Month 1					
Month 2					
Month 3					
				Multiply three months and subtract 1	

In closing, I recommend calculating a return for your account *in aggregate*. This means adding all your accounts together and treating them as one account for the purpose of calculating your return. This gives you an idea of the total performance of the portfolio, not just the performance of specific accounts. In aggregate, it is the total return where the performance gap becomes most prevalent.

Appendix II

Stock Picking as a Hobby

This book has taken all the fun out of investing in the stock market, so now let's put some back in. Appendix II refers to stock picking as a hobby, which I believe it should be. To make stock picking a hobby, you need a small brokerage account funded with money that will not make or break you. It is just as exciting and more fun playing the market with a little bit of money than with a larger portion of your savings.

I have a small account that I call bingo money in memory of my late Grandma Ferri. While washing clothes, she frequently found spare change in my grandfather's pants. That money went into a special jar labeled "Bingo Money." Every Monday night she took the jar to the local church to play bingo. She never won a lot, she never lost a lot, but she had a great time.

Your "bingo" account should be used specifically for the purpose of choosing stocks. Playing the market should be limited to the small amount of money in the account. I suggest opening an account with a witty stockbroker, someone who is pleasant to talk to and will pick up the phone when you call. Don't worry about paying regular commission rates. The cost of commissions is your least worry in this account. You will have a hard enough time trying to pick a few winners. Inform your broker that you have no interest in buying packaged products or insurance. That way you will not be approached with the latest limited partnership or other investment gimmick.

When you are ready to invest there are thousands of stock strategies to try. You can buy growth, value, small-cap, or momentum stocks; it really does not matter. Chances are you will flip from one strategy to another over time. Of course it is always better to stick with one strategy. That is how truly gifted stock investors become wealthy. But 99.9% of stock investors are not gifted, and their chance of success in any strategy is slim. Therefore, I recommend trying different ideas until you find a style you enjoy and understand. I do not recommend trading futures or options since the money can disappear too fast.

Tips on Using Brokerage Research

When you start working with a brokerage house, you will likely be introduced to stock ideas that have recently been touted by the firm's analysts. Unless these are household names like AT&T, Cola-Cola, or Microsoft, there are a few things you need to know about Wall Street recommendations.

The Real Prize—Investment Banking Fees

Assume your broker calls to recommend a certain small stock that his firm just placed on their "buy list." The broker says the firm believes the stock offers superior investment potential and that the analyst is highly recommending the company. Should you believe this story? Maybe, and maybe not. Before we go any further, you need to know something about the real job of stock analysts and brokerage firms.

Stock analysts at brokerage firms wear many hats and serve many masters, but the master who speaks louder than all others is the *Investment Banking* master. When a brokerage firm acts as an underwriter for a company issuing new stocks or bonds, the firm makes a handsome investment banking fee. The analyst plays an important role in bringing in the investment banking clients and selling the new securities.

During a typical day analysts attend meetings, write research reports, talk to the press, speak at various functions, and do a variety of other things. They also keep current on the companies they follow. As a rule, analysts are obligated to cover the biggest companies in their industry, such as those in the S&P 500. After covering the "big boys," they don't have a lot of time to look for promising young companies.

Generally, analysts will *not* recommend small companies merely because they believe the stock price will go up. As a rule, there must be an investment banking relationship or potential relationship for an analyst to take notice of a small company. A smaller firm may have a wonderful income statement, a fantastic balance sheet, and tremendous potential for growth, but if the company is not looking to issue new stocks or bonds from a Wall Street brokerage firm, few analysts bother to issue research reports or put them on the buy list.

In addition, stock analysts tend to increase their coverage of large companies who are currently in need of investment banking. A study by Columbia University concluded that Wall Street analysts generally provide greater coverage to investment banking clients and give them higher ratings overall.[74] Paying for coverage and

---

74. Warren Boeker and Matthew Hayward, Columbia University Graduate School of Business, 1996

high ratings through investment banking fees is the nature of Wall Street. It has always been this way, and always will be.

How does this conflict of interest affect you as an individual investor? Don't buy a stock if your brokerage firm is involved in the underwriting, especially of a small company. Typically, a buy recommendation from a broker participating in a company's financial strategies will trail the stock market. One study found that stock recommendations relating to an investment banking relationship underperformed the market by a 14% over a two-year period following the offering. In contrast, recommendations of analysts not involved in the relationship outperformed the market by 32% over the same period.[75]

When a broker calls to pitch an unfamiliar stock, experienced investors learn to ask if an investment banking relationship exists. The broker is obligated to disclose the relationship if there is one. Unless you are familiar with the company from an unbiased source, I recommend avoiding stocks if a banking relationship exists between the broker and the stock.

The Bottom Line

How good is all Wall Street research? According to *The Wall Street Journal*, most analysts might as well be throwing darts. The *Journal* tracks the performance of analysts' recommendations from various brokerage firms and publishes the results on a regular basis. For a five-year period ending June 30, 1998, ten out of fifteen brokerage firms surveyed were not able to achieve the returns of the S&P 500.[76] These results did not include

75. Roni Michaely and Kent L. Womack, "Conflict of Interest and the Credibility of Underwriters Analysts' Recommendation," preliminary paper Sunriver Oregon, June 19-22, 1996

trading costs, which would have lowered the reported returns.

Picking stocks should be a hobby, and only hobby money should be used for playing the market. Your serious stock money should be in index funds as discussed in Chapter 12. If you are interested in learning about stocks, read a few good books on the subject and take a couple of college courses. Have fun, be safe, and don't confuse brains with a bull market.

---

76. Gorgette Jason, "The Pros Give Up Some Bragging Rights", *The Wall Street Journal*, July 21, 1998, C1, Stock returns were based on each firms recommended list.

Appendix III

Beware of Brokers Bearing Asset Allocation Advice

$\mathbf{A}$sset allocation modeling is a relatively simple idea based on sound academic theory. Research tell us that by diversifying a portfolio into several asset classes, such as stocks and bonds, you can increase your return and control your risk. But there are limitations that need to be addressed when using an asset allocation model to determine the mix of assets in your portfolio. Many of these limitations are not readily apparent, especially to the large number of financial advisors who use their models to sell investment products.

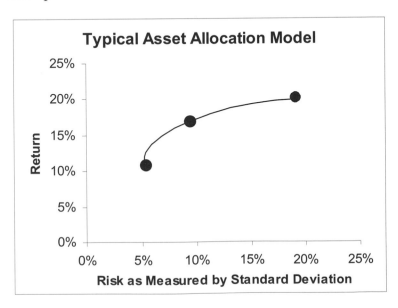

Model Risk and Investor Risk

The previous chart is a sample asset allocation model. It shows the risk and return of several stock and bond market mixes over the last fifteen years. On the left side of the model is the rate of return, and on the bottom is a measure of portfolio risk. The strong bull market of the 1980s and 1990s caused people to focus on the left side of this asset allocation model, the rate of return. Equally as important, though often neglected in a bull market, is the risk of the portfolio. The concept of risk is one of the most misunderstood and mismanaged areas in the investment advice industry.

Asset allocation theory has become deeply imbedded in the mass market for financial products. Almost all financial advisors have some form or model at their fingertips. Asset allocation theory was originally developed for use by institutional investors. For this reason, the calculation to assess risk was fairly complex. Institutions measure risk by standard deviation, or the variability of portfolio returns over long periods of time.

Institutional investors understand the basic concept of using standard deviation as a measure of risk. Unfortunately, the public does not. Standard deviation does not adequately reflect short-term volatility that occurs in the markets, which is precisely the kind of risk that affects individual investor behavior. When the markets become volatile in the short term, people lose money. Since the average investor thinks about risk in terms of losing money or running out of money during retirement, he or she tends to act impulsively to change their allocation.[77] Long-term models, such as the one in the previous chart, assume that an investor will not change

---

77. John L. Maginn and Donald L. Tuttle, *Managing Investment Portfolios,* 2nd Edition, Warren, Gorham, & Lamont, 1990, pg. 3-2

the allocation over a very long period of time. If an investor does not maintain a stable asset mix, he or she is in danger of reducing their exposure to stocks at the wrong time. In other words, they start trying to time the markets.

Other Institutional Terms

Statistical tools such as standard deviation, optimization, and utility are important theoretical concepts used at high levels of academic research. However, many advisors who use these terms to sell investment products misunderstand the concepts. One reason for their lack of understanding is due to a lack of training in the investment industry. Statistical concepts are taught at colleges and universities, and as we learned in Chapter 7, most advisors have a limited education outside of their firm. If an advisor does not fully understand the statistical concepts in the model, he tends to recommend portfolios that are too risky for his clients. This leaves investors open to poor portfolio returns as they bail out of a bad market.

Nominal Returns and Real Returns

Most asset allocation models used in marketing brochure and other sales materials look like the first chart in this appendix. They use *nominal* rates of returns. The returns are not adjusted for *inflation*. In other words, the model includes the inflation rate as part of the return, which causes investors to have unrealistic expectations about their future returns. For example, from 1973 to 1997 a conservative portfolio of 50% stocks and 50% bonds would have earned a return of 11%. Adjusted for inflation, however, the return was reduced to 5.5%.

Using nominal returns distorts reality. Investors and advisors should be using an asset allocation model that adjusts for the inflation rate, such as the one in the following chart.

Inflation Adjusted Market Returns

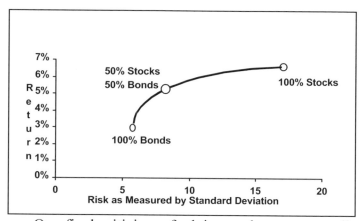

One final criticism of advisors who use asset allocation models to sell investment products is that most models are based on the return of a market index and not the returns of actively managed products sold by advisors. As a result, the model in no way reflects the return an investor would have achieved in an actively managed account, especially after fees. Although index funds are a logical fit for portfolios based on asset allocation models, most advisors want no part of this approach because an advisor receives little compensation for selling index funds. I personally believe that using index returns to sell active products is unethical. Advisors *bait* investors with models showing index fund returns, then *switch* to high-cost active management. This tactic once again shows that most people in the industry exist to make money from you, not for you.

In summary, the returns of asset allocation models overstate the return to investors and understate the risks. Many advisors who use the models to sell investment products don't really understand the statistics behind them, but use them anyway to push products with higher fees. In a bear market, most portfolios based on faulty allocations assumptions break down as investors' true risk tolerance levels are exposed.

INDEX